The Law Into Their Own Hands

# The Law Into Their Own Hands

Immigration and the Politics of Exceptionalism

Roxanne Lynn Doty

The University of Arizona Press     Tucson

The University of Arizona Press
© 2009 The Arizona Board of Regents

Library of Congress Cataloging-in-Publication Data

Doty, Roxanne Lynn.
    The law into their own hands : immigration and the
politics of exceptionalism / Roxanne Lynn Doty.
        p. cm.
    Includes bibliographical references and index.
    ISBN 978-0-8165-2770-0 (hardcover : alk. paper) —
    ISBN 978-0-8165-2771-7 (pbk. : alk. paper)
    1. Illegal aliens—United States.   2. Militia movements—
United States.   3. Border patrols—Mexican-American
Border Region.   4. Border security—Mexican-American
Border Region.   5. Vigilantes—Mexican-American Border
Region.   6. United States—Race relations.   7. Hate—
United States.   8. United States—Emigration and
immigration.   I. Title.
JV6565.D68 2009
325.73—dc22 2008031517


Manufactured in the United States of America on acid-free,
archival-quality paper containing a minimum of 50% post-
consumer waste and processed chlorine free.


14   13   12   11   10   09      6   5   4   3   2   1

# Contents

# Acknowledgments

Portions of research for this book were presented at the Western Social Science Association Conference in Phoenix, Arizona, in April 2006 and at the International Studies Association Conference in Chicago, Illinois, in March 2007. I would like to thank discussants and audience members for their comments and suggestions. I would also like to thank the three anonymous reviewers from University of Arizona Press for their extremely insightful readings and valuable suggestions.

In the course of my research for this book, I have had the honor of meeting some individuals who work tirelessly for the rights of migrants and present a hopeful counter to the sentiments of the anti-immigrant movement. I dedicate this book and a portion of the proceeds to two such groups, Humane Borders and No Más Muertes.

# The Law Into Their Own Hands

# 1
# Fear and Loathing on the U.S.-Mexico Border

## The Minuteman Project, April 2005

> If this were Crawford, TX, the Marines would be here.[1]

The *Tombstone Tumbleweed* newspaper office is a tiny, one-story house with an old-fashioned front porch and small yard surrounded by a white picket fence. This little structure, which is located at 312 Toughnut Street in Tombstone, Arizona, serves as headquarters for the Minuteman Project (MMP), a civilian border patrol group founded in October 2004 by retired California businessman Jim Gilchrist and Chris Simcox, owner and editor of the *Tombstone Tumbleweed*. A wanted poster of the 9/11 hijackers is taped to the outside of the door, compliments of Veterans for Secure Borders. Next to this poster is another with photos of Pima County, Arizona's most wanted, all burly-looking young men with Hispanic surnames. The intent behind this juxtaposition is obvious.[2] Inside, the office is a bustle of activity and clutter of papers. The phone rings incessantly. A poster hangs on the wall displaying the following words in large, bold black letters against a white background: "Article IV, Section 4 of the U.S. Constitution—Every State in this Union shall be protected against invasion—Protect U.S. Citizens—Secure Our Borders." Next to this poster is a painting of controversial, conservative political commentator Ann Coulter.

I first visit the newspaper office on April 16, 2005, when the MMP is in full swing.[3] A man who calls himself Grey Deacon runs the office and answers the phone.[4] Chris Simcox is out in "the field" with a group of new recruits.

"It's been ringing off the hook," Deacon says, glancing at the phone. "And we get hundreds of e-mails from people supporting us."

Deacon has strong views about undocumented migrants and strenuously objects to the terms "undocumented immigrant" and "illegal immigrant."

"They're not immigrants," he insists. "They're illegal *aliens*."

He also has some opinions about Mexico that he is eager to share. He compares Vicente Fox and the Mexican government to Saddam Hussein's Iraq. I am tempted to engage him on this point, but I hold my tongue. I'm not here to debate. MMP recruits are signing up in the backyard, and Deacon tells me there will be an orientation later in the afternoon at the Palominas Trading Post that I am welcome to attend. When I leave, Deacon walks to the door with me, pauses at the posters of Pima County's most wanted and the 9/11 hijackers, and points hard at them with his index finger. "That's why we're here," he says with an air of patriotic pride, full of mission and purpose. I fight the urge to ask if he is aware of the fact that none of the 9/11 hijackers entered the United States through the U.S.-Mexico border.

The Palominas Trading Post is about forty miles from Tombstone on Highway 92, a two-lane road in southern Arizona that parallels the border for several miles before curving north to Sierra Vista. Palominas is a few miles west of the turn-off for the Naco Highway, which runs for about twenty miles into the tiny, ghost-like, unincorporated town of Naco, Arizona, bordering Naco, Mexico. The Trading Post itself is an experience, a combination of small-town America and Wild West outpost complete with blowing tumbleweeds and swirling dust devils dancing across the highway. A string of tiny, twinkling lights hangs from the eaves. The people inside the Trading Post, which is really a small café with an assortment of trinkets, cigarettes, and basic groceries for sale, are a mixture of grandfatherly-looking old men, young and middle-aged men wearing "undocumented border patrol" T-shirts, and a few middle-aged women. The action is outside, though. Chris Simcox and Mike Gaddy, a MMP section leader, are sitting on a large, oblong water tank. Anti-immigrant activist Russell Dove wears an American flag bandana and black shirt with "U.S. Constitution Enforcement" in bold yellow letters across the back.[5] An assortment of RVs, trucks, cars, and tents are scattered in the desert next to and behind the Trading Post. About thirty people, most of whom are recruits, and a few media people are assembled in the clearing in front of Simcox and Gaddy. Simcox welcomes them and tells them about this weekend's operations. He is younger than I expected (mid-forties), and except for the "United Patriots of America" baseball cap he is wearing, nothing would give him away as a border vigilante. He is not armed and, dressed in pale blue jeans and a grayish blue sweatshirt, he looks more like the elementary school teacher he used to be than any stereotype of someone who has issued a "call to arms" for a citizen's militia. Simcox tells the volunteers about the thousands of supportive e-mails he has received and the manual the MMP is putting together, as well as their plans for a four-border-state operation in the fall. His words generate vigorous applause. A plane flies overhead and he tells us that it is one of three currently in the air that have been brought to the area by owners who are MMP volunteers. An atmosphere of excitement permeates the group. Some audience members have weapons, some do not. The group divides itself up to caravan out to the various "positions" where Minutemen volunteers are stationed.

I follow Mike Gaddy to the "Huachuca Line," which consists of eleven observation points strung out along an approximately two-mile stretch of Highway 92. MMP volunteers have fanned out along these points beginning at mile marker 331, positioning themselves about twenty to thirty feet from the highway in an area characterized by semi-desert scrub and thin woods. An American flag flies at the "entrance" to positions five and six, which consist of two campsites amongst a thin cluster of trees that break the intensity of the sun and provide a partial shield from the highway. Mike Gaddy, or Sergeant Major as he is called by the volunteers, describes how migrants (he uses the word "illegals") come through the Huachuca Mountains, cross the highway, and head west to Hereford Road where the "coyotes" or smugglers pick them up. There are many washes and other places to hide in this area, especially under cover of darkness. The task of the volunteers is to watch for the "illegals" and report them to the Border Patrol.

There are long periods of boredom, Gaddy says, when nothing is happening. "Then you spot an illegal and the adrenaline starts pumping." The rush of blood through veins, the quickening of pulses is almost palpable here in this remote corner of the world. Identifying a "target," which is the word Gaddy uses to refer to a migrant, is what makes the hours of tedium worthwhile. It's sort of like being in combat infantry, he says. Gaddy is a thirty-year Army veteran of Vietnam, Grenada, and Beirut. He is a pleasant, ruddy-complexioned man with a short, stubbly, grayish white beard and mustache. He wears a camouflage hat and green Army fatigue pants. He's a no-nonsense sort of guy and speaks with confidence. The volunteers treat him with deference. "Sergeant Major, have you mentioned the rattlesnakes?" they ask, or, "Sergeant Major, have you told them about hydrating?" Sergeant Major graciously acknowledges these reminders: "Use lots of ChapStick. Don't lick your lips.

The critters will usually leave you alone if you don't bother them." His tone is imbued with the kind of self-assurance that comes from understanding that you are on a mission, undertaking a task that some do not have the guts to do, and from knowing precisely and with certainty just who you are and who "they" are. This self-assurance pervades the atmosphere.

A young ex-Marine from Mesa, Arizona—about 250 miles from here —who has been on the line for the weekend, tells me what a great time he has had. What neat people he has met. When I ask him why he is armed, he says it's for protection. He says there have been threats. He says the smugglers are dangerous. And besides, there are rattlesnakes out here. There is an overweight woman in her mid-forties standing next to an overweight man I presume is her husband. She announces they'll be coming to this spot for the night with a camper and she'll make coffee for everyone in the morning. Another woman, who looks to be in her seventies, wears sandals and thin cotton pants with a matching top. Dainty, heart-shaped gold earrings glitter on her ears.[6] Gaddy tells the group to caravan with him to one more position that might be a bit hard to find and gives directions to the other spots. "Pick out one you like," he says. "Then get your stuff and set up camp." In closing, he says, "Enjoy yourself. You're protecting America." On the way back to Tombstone, I pass a middle-aged couple, wearing sun hats and no doubt swathed in sunscreen, sitting in lawn chairs along Highway 92, watching for migrants. A whole other cadre of concerned Americans is positioned along Border Road a few yards from Mexico.

## The Significance of Civilian Border Groups

Are these people to be taken seriously? I asked myself this question over and over in April 2005. At times, I found it hard to fathom that the assortment of people I observed then and subsequently could possibly constitute something worth more attention and study. There was a big element of "show" evident in the April 2005 Minuteman Project, as well as in other border watches and internal operations. It would be easy to dismiss the whole phenomenon as farce and the groups as ridiculous, disgruntled fringe elements in a society experiencing complex and rapid transformations within the context of an increasingly interconnected world. I was tempted to do so, but hesitated. The MMP and other civilian border patrol groups that have formed in recent years are part of a larger phenomenon of anti-immigrant groups, not all of which engage in the physical patrolling of the border, but whose existence revolves around the concept of borders and the fear that borders are not quite as secure, fixed in meaning, and impermeable as might have once been thought. This concern is shared by many policy makers and numerous scholars in various fields in the social sciences. As undocumented immigration has become an increasingly prominent issue, individual citizens have responded to calls from private groups such as the Minuteman Project to take action.[7] Reports suggest that membership and donations to civilian border groups as well as other anti-immigrant organizations have increased dramatically.[8] These groups have spread beyond border states and even into traditionally progressive areas such as the San Francisco Bay area.[9] But while this phenomenon has received an overwhelming amount of national and international media attention, as well as attention from rights groups and policy makers, there is no detailed, systematic, descriptive examination of this issue that is also theoretically informed and conceptually sophisticated. A recent Congressional Research Service memo to the U.S. House Committee on the Judiciary had to rely primarily on press reports because of the lack of scholarly as well as government sources.[10]

How do we understand civilian border groups? What are their connections to the broader anti-immigrant movement and other societal groups? Civilian border groups do not arise and exist in isolation. One of the reasons for their significance is that they are connected to other groups, either directly or indirectly, intentionally or unintentionally. Nor are they without social and political significance. The very fact that they have received such widespread attention would seem to suggest that they have some significance, if only by virtue of this attention. This book argues, though, that the significance of these groups is more than just a media creation. Their existence and the practices they engage in have important implications for what are generally regarded as foundational principles that are at the heart of democratic political orders, principles that face challenges in the context of a world characterized by more porous borders and relative ease of movement.[11] Undocumented migration raises fundamental questions about law and order and thus about the state and its willingness and ability to effectively control who crosses its sovereign territorial borders. Border vigilante groups, who claim that the state has failed to adequately protect its borders—and has thus abrogated its duty to provide order and security for its citizens—highlight the role of the populace in enforcing the law or at least demanding its enforcement. The former is an issue of *state sovereignty*; the latter calls our attention to *popular sovereignty*. These two concepts are deeply embedded in political theory as well as in political practice. They are also key to civilian border groups. The concept of sovereignty and related ideas are thus important in broaching an understanding of this phenomenon and are discussed below.

Civilian border groups have arisen within a social and political context that has enabled them to blossom and gain a significant degree of legitimacy. It is important to examine this context, which includes the contemporary anti-immigrant movement of which these groups form a part, as well as other groups whose primary focus is not immigration but who have forged links with the anti-immigrant movement. In addition to the relationship between civilian border patrol groups and the broader anti-immigrant movement, this study explores three additional connections: the national security connection, the white supremacist/nativist connection, and the Christian right connection.

First, the linking of immigration issues with national security has figured prominently in the ways in which the former is understood and acted upon.[12] National security is one of the most talked-about contemporary issues and has spurred numerous government policies and laws, many of which are connected to immigration. While the major focus of this study is not immigration and national security per se, I would be remiss to ignore how civilian border and anti-immigrants groups have appropriated issues of national security and how this has functioned to make their messages resonate with other social and political groups.

Next, white supremacist groups have a long history of opposition to immigrants. So, in one respect, they share a "natural" affinity with civilian border groups. According to the Southern Poverty Law Center, the number of extremist nativist groups has increased by 40 percent since 2000. Much of this growth has been driven by opposition to immigration. While not all nativists explicitly espouse the racist ideology of neo-Nazi organizations, some certainly do.[13] Thus, it is important to carefully examine empirical evidence that points to connections between these groups and the anti-immigrant movement.

Finally, while the connection with the Christian right is one that I was not aware of when I began this project, it surfaced in the course of my research and is included here because it is potentially significant in the sense that it provides another channel through which anti-immigrant sentiments and messages can be disseminated and legitimated.

Anti-immigrant sentiment runs high in the United States today. Wayne A. Cornelius (2005) has suggested that this sentiment is broad but not very deep. This may be the case if "deep" is measured as "salience" through the employment of survey research methodologies. However, I would argue that survey research may fail to capture the depth of anti-immigrant sentiment, which can manifest itself in numerous ways and whose salience may vary across locales. A poll conducted in the state of Arizona by the Walter Cronkite School of Journalism and KAET public television in January 2007 found that undocumented immigration was the single most important problem that respondents thought the state legislature needed to address.[14] This does not necessarily indicate the way in which Arizonans think this issue should be dealt with, but subsequent polls (see chapter 5), as well as citizen and voter action, have made it clear that anti-immigrant sentiment is broad and deep in that state. The important thing here is that this sentiment is subject to manipulation at the hands of well-organized anti-immigrant groups and local leaders.[15]

## Sovereignty, Security, and the Politics of Exceptionalism

> The high points of politics are simultaneously the moments in
> which the enemy is, in concrete clarity, recognized as the enemy.
> (Schmitt, 1996: 67)

That "immigration policy is deeply embedded in the question of state sovereignty" seems indisputable.[16] The ways in which sovereignty are addressed by scholars who study immigration is sometimes direct, while for others it is more implicit. For example, the "gap hypothesis," which addresses the significant chasm between official immigration policies and the actual outcome of these policies, implicitly invokes the issue of state sovereignty in that such a gap calls into question the ability of the state to control its sovereign territorial borders.[17] Other hypotheses deal more directly with the issue of state sovereignty, suggesting that immigration-related legal decisions dilute it by simultaneously devaluing citizenship and giving priority to international human rights law.[18] Peter Andreas (2000) emphasizes the complex relationship between the sovereign state and practices that on the surface seem to undermine sovereignty—but which upon closer analysis are dependent on the state, tolerated and often encouraged by it. While scholars may differ on the precise relationship between sovereignty and immigration, there is agreement that sovereignty is a key element and is arguably at the heart of undocumented migration as a political and legal issue. If not for the widely recognized sovereign right of states to determine and control who is permitted to cross their borders, to work, and to take up residence within their sovereign territory, undocumented migration would have little significance. In a world of no borders and free movement, this topic would be irrelevant.[19]

Clearly, the centrality of sovereignty is not only recognized by scholars of immigration, but is a prominent theme with civilian border groups as well. A key philosophical underpinning of all the contemporary border vigilante groups as well as earlier vigilante movements is the idea of popular sovereignty. The notion that the legitimacy of a ruler (or the state) is to be found in "the people" who are the source of sovereignty is shared across a broad spectrum of citizens who may differ radically in many other aspects of their political beliefs and ideologies.[20]

My concern in this study is not to engage debates on the challenges migration presents for state sovereignty or to "bring the state back" into the analysis. Sufficient attention has already been given to these issues by those noted above. Instead, I focus on two specific and related elements of sovereignty originally suggested by legal scholar Carl Schmitt: the friend-enemy distinction and the *politics of exceptionalism* that follows from this distinction.[21] *Exceptionalism* refers to those political situations in which individuals and groups are turned into an *exception* by the exercise of sovereign power, resulting in their exclusion from basic rights guaranteed by the law or the constitution. Such exclusions create extreme vulnerabilities for those affected. Political theorists such as Giorgio Agamden (2005) consider Nazi concentration camps to be the most prominent example of exceptionalism. The term, though, refers to a much broader phenomenon than has generally been considered and is not limited to practices of the sovereign state conceived as a unitary, cohesive entity.

Exceptionalism can be enacted at various levels of government: federal, state, and local. In addition, citizens can engage in a politics of exceptionalism that feeds into official government action, in which case the sovereignty of the state and popular sovereignty become inextricably linked to one another. Popular sovereignty functions as a source of legitimation for civilian border groups and provides justification for their practices. However, exercises of popular sovereignty on the part of citizen border groups are ultimately aimed at the state, which they claim has failed "the people." In essence, they are demanding that the state be more sovereign, that it forcefully exercise its sovereignty by controlling its borders and making *exceptions* of those who have entered the United States without the proper documentation. This study critically examines, within the context of the contemporary "immigration crises," how the two elements of sovereignty (the friend-enemy distinction and exceptionalism) are played out in numerous practices, and with what consequences. I argue that the major consequence is an increasingly bifurcated society that is structured along the lines of the exception. This politics of exceptionalism has resulted in widespread and focused attention on distinctions between citizens and noncitizens, which in turn legitimates the exclusion and marginalization of some and quite often entails a demonization of noncitizens. I suggest that the contemporary politics of exceptionalism is practiced by numerous members of society and is not limited to government officials. The practices of civilian border groups and those connected to them are instances of this.

The whole array of activities engaged in by civilian border groups and the anti-immigrant movement are examples of a politics of exceptionalism. Essential to this is the production and reproduction of the friend-enemy distinction. For Carl Schmitt, this distinction is the characteristic of "the political" that allows this realm to be distinguished from others, such as the legal realm, the moral realm, the economic realm, and the aesthetic realm. Each of these other realms has their own defining logics and distinctions. The economic realm is defined to a large extent by the profitable versus the unprofitable, the aesthetic realm by the beautiful versus the ugly, and the moral realm by good versus evil. While the political can draw upon these other distinctions for support and the enemy can easily be treated as evil and/or ugly, this does not alter the autonomy of the distinctions. For Schmitt, "the specific political distinction to which political actions and motives can be reduced is that between friend and enemy" (1996: 26). It makes sense that this fundamental distinction is an essential element of sovereignty. While discussions of sovereignty do not always explicitly refer to the friend-enemy distinction, the opposition nonetheless forms a silent backdrop for almost any issue in which questions of sovereignty are raised, and most certainly when it comes to the issue of undocumented immigration.[22] Lines of delineation between peoples, whether territorial lines or other kinds of divisions, can be powerful symbolic representations of the distinction between friends and potential enemies. The notion of an "us" versus "them" is not new and is arguably inherent in the very concept of a nation and national identity. It can reasonably be suggested that nations need enemies, at least in terms of how nations have historically been understood and in terms of the practices they have engaged in to perpetuate their existence.

Schmitt is important because he gives this notion a central position in defining the concept of sovereignty and in understanding the practices associated with it. Importantly, the enemy does not need to be hated personally, nor must the enemy be morally evil or aesthetically ugly or an economic competitor. What the enemy must be is "the other, the stranger; and it is sufficient for his nature that he is, in an especially intense way, existentially something different and alien, so that in the extreme case conflicts with him are possible" (Schmitt, 1996: 27). Schmitt goes on to say: "The enemy is solely the public enemy, because everything that has a relationship to such a collectivity of men, particularly to a whole nation, becomes public by virtue of such a relationship" (Schmitt, 1996: 28).

One of the major effects of civilian border groups as well as of the anti-immigrant movement is to bring into clear focus whom they presume is the enemy. While the practices and rhetoric of some border vigilantes may seem to verge on personal hatred, this is not always the case, nor are such instances of personal hatred what makes border vigilantes socially and politically relevant. It is the public nature that is key. To be clear, I am not suggesting that the civilian border groups bring to our attention the identity of an enemy in any objective sense. I am not suggesting that they do society a service by making us aware of an enemy that we were not cognizant of before. Their practices (which would include their rhetorical practices such as the slogans on the signs displayed at rallies) have the effect of *socially constructing* an enemy who presents a danger to the social order. This gives rise to and justifies practices (and policies) that otherwise would fly in the face of most of our notions of democracy and human/civil rights. While it is undoubtedly true that Nazi Germany's policies towards the Jewish populations of Europe constitute an extreme example of exceptionalism, Jef Huysmans (2004: 321–341) points out that exceptionalism often enters the "judicial, societal, economic, and political fabric" in ways less spectacular than expressions such as detainment and extermination camps. It would be a serious mistake to ignore the seemingly less extraordinary enactments of exceptionalism, for they can illuminate a great deal about this phenomenon and they have serious consequences for those whose lives are affected. It is my contention that the civilian border patrol phenomenon, the anti-immigration movement, and the policies pertaining to undocumented immigration are linked to constitute contemporary forms of exceptionalism and that they are vitally important in their implications for a democratic political order. Exceptionalism, as a concept grounded in concrete social and political practices, has serious implications for how we think about the basic rights and duties that are part of such an order. This concept provides a conceptual thread that weaves through the ideas and related practices that have taken place over the past few years and that have been directed towards undocumented migrants.

Exceptionalism, as manifested in the subject matter examined here, is intricately connected to the notion of *societal security*, which articulates a conceptualization of security that is not subsumed under state security as conventionally understood and thus calls attention to a broader range of phenomena that affect the security (or presumed security) of collectivities.[23] Societal security is meant to capture a societal group's concern about their survival as an entity, such as a nation or an ethic or religious group. When such societal groups perceive a threat to their security, a sense of emergency is generated and with it a willingness to take extraordinary emergency measures. The forms that "emergency measures" take can, of course, vary tremendously depending on the situation. Groups can take the law into their own hands in a variety of ways. They can offer their assistance to legal authorities. They can be violent or nonviolent. They can engage in symbolic practices in efforts to prompt the state to take action. Societal security highlights the fact that pronouncements of security concerns are not solely the purview of state actors.

Civilian border patrol groups have engaged in a variety of practices that demonstrate their concern with the presumed eroding of societal security, most notably their highly visible and well-publicized patrols at various locations along the U.S.-Mexico border, which have been symbolic as well as both nonviolent and violent.[24] For border vigilantes and the anti-immigrant movement, societal security is at the heart of their concerns with immigrants and especially the undocumented who are already in the United States. Their construction of the enemy, to a large extent, revolves around their societal insecurity.

National security also enters the picture in important ways and is intricately woven into societal security. This is evident in the concern with terrorism and arguments that "terrorists love open borders," which is ostensibly a national security issue but quickly becomes an instance of societal security when specific groups/peoples are presumed to be connected or at least potentially connected to terrorism and thus deemed potential threats to "our way of life" and "our identity as a nation." The numerous banners displayed at anti-immigrant gatherings as well as in the rhetoric of leaders of civilian border groups that link terrorism and national security to open borders illustrate this.[25] The concern with societal security is also manifest in more subtle ways and can be found in sophisticated and nuanced arguments that resonate with a broad audience not limited to civilian border groups or even members of the anti-immigrant movement. Culture and values are prominent concerns expressed in contemporary discussions of immigration and are generally articulated around the idea of assimilation. Whether intentionally or not, this becomes an important element in distinguishing self from other and can work to construct the unassimilated other as a danger to society and thus at least a potential enemy. The concept of assimilation functions within a context of both societal and national security and can be implicated in the construction of the friend-enemy distinction. This becomes part of the overall social context within which civilian border control groups operate and achieve legitimacy.

The concept of vigilantism is also pertinent to this study. Vigilantism is generally considered a domestic/national phenomenon and has received very little attention from scholars of international politics or global studies. However, border groups, such as the Minutemen, make it clear that vigilantism is not simply a local or national phenomenon, but rather is inextricably linked to the global. The Mexican government has expressed concern on numerous occasions regarding the activities of civilian border groups in the United States, making this an issue that transcends national borders.[26] Vigilantism, in this instance, links up with issues of societal security and provides an additional conceptual tool for understanding civilian border groups and the context within which they function. While the term *vigilante* is controversial and difficult to define in a rigorous social scientific manner, it is useful because vigilante groups fit into a long history—especially in the United States—of extra-legal groups that form in response to what they regard as a breakdown of law and order. Richard Maxwell Brown defines vigilante groups as "organized extra-legal movements the members of which take the law into their own hands" and also as "associations in which citizens have joined together for self-protection under conditions of disorder."[27] Civilian border patrol groups seek to redress a perceived inadequacy in, or lack of enforcement of, existing law. While not all of them engage in overt acts of physical violence, there have been such instances and the threat of violence always lurks, especially when members are armed, as they often are.[28]

Vigilantism can inform and enhance our understanding of the ways in which exceptionalism comes into being. It calls attention to a more complicated picture of the ways in which decisions regarding friends and enemies take place. We are compelled to ask what it means to "decide." What happens when "the decision" slips from the firm grip of the state and/or elite members of society positioned in powerful institutions? Vigilantism, in the form of civilian border patrol groups, raises questions about the relationship between official decisions and the myriad decisions that often precede them, as well as between the "private" realm of citizen action and the "public" realm of official, government-sanctioned action. Examining numerous, seemingly small, and local decisions shifts our attention from "the state" as it is narrowly conceived to more amorphous realms, in which the sensibilities, ideologies, desires, and numerous other forces that support "the state" and are arguably essential for it to thrive—or even to exist—are played out. I refer to the subject of this refocusing as "statecraft from below."[29]

This concept suggests that we may need to rethink dominant understandings of how sovereign authority and power work, and where or in whom they are located. It forces us to consider that not only is "the state" not a unitary, rational, and cohesive entity, but it also may not have a monopoly on practices that construct the friend-enemy distinction and exceptions. What if "the state" is not the only site of the "sovereign decision" of the exception and the enemy? What if this is a widely dispersed and at times amorphous phenomenon not controlled or even initiated by elites and/or policy makers? Arguably, in some cases, "the decision" regarding the enemy and the exception is not one decision at all, but many decisions that may have already been made long before official decisions are reached. Sensitivity to these "what-ifs" speaks to the issue of the relationship between the theoretical and the concrete. The concrete case here both grounds and informs the abstract conceptual tools brought to bear.

The phenomenon under investigation here also raises fundamental questions about "the decision" itself as a concept. Does "the decision" have to be one to suspend the normal operations of the law, as Carl Schmitt suggests, or can it be to invigorate or re-enforce the law or change the law in such a way so as to preserve a particular understanding of "the social order"? Can it be a decision to take the law into one's own hands? I argue that it is more accurate to think of numerous and widely dispersed decisions that both individually and collectively serve to create "exceptional" life situations for some human beings and structure society in ways that raise important questions about what it means to be a democracy and to value human beings who are members of the community. This study examines an array of such decisions that have been made over the past few years that can reasonably be connected to the increased attention to undocumented migration brought on in large part by the overwhelming amount of attention given to the Minuteman Project, its offshoots, other border groups, and the ready acceptance of their cause by policy makers and social and political groups. Some of these decisions are local, some are regional, some are national. Some have received little publicity; others have garnered a great deal of press coverage. Some of the examples are from the state of Arizona. This is reasonable because so much of the anti-immigrant activity in the United States has taken place in Arizona, though it is by no means unique, and though some of the decisions that have much significance for the lives and futures of those humans beings who bear the label "undocumented" have taken place far from the actual territorial border areas in the United States.

This is not the first time in history that immigration has elicited negative reactions from some segments of the population.[30] That fact, however, does not make the current situation any less important. Clearly, there are unique aspects of the contemporary immigration issue and the responses it has elicited. One of these is the sheer number of civilian border vigilantes and grassroots anti-immigrant groups. Another is the use of modern technology and communication tools by anti-immigrant activists, which have enabled them to connect with one another and thus has lent strength to the overall movement. My goal is not to unduly exaggerate the consequences of civilian border patrols and the anti-immigrant movement. The point I wish to stress is that there have been many dispersed decisions (local, national, official, and unofficial) made by numerous individuals and collectivities that have had real consequences for the lives of those migrants who are affected by them. Focusing on a multiplicity of decisions, some of which are very localized, speaks directly to the issue of where we look for political practices that create lines of distinction between members of communities and construct some individuals and groups as enemies.

In chapter 2, I examine the rise of contemporary civilian border groups as well as their historical predecessors. I view these through the conceptual lenses discussed above. Specifically, I show how civilian border groups can be placed within a long tradition of vigilantism in the United States. In chapter 3, I place these groups within the context of the broader anti-immigrant movement and illustrate the important connections between border vigilantes and the larger movement. This chapter also examines the linkages between the anti-immigrant movement and other societal groups with whom their concerns and themes resonate. As noted above, an important feature of the anti-immigrant movement has been its ability to forge connections with other groups whose main concerns are not necessarily immigration, but who have taken up the cause. These include linkages between (1) immigration and national security, (2) connections to white supremacist/nativist groups, and (3) the Christian right connection.

The ways in which the messages of the civilian border groups have been disseminated are the subject of chapter 4. The messages of groups such as the Minutemen have been cheered by white supremacists, talk-radio hosts, and cable television, as well as ostensibly more respectable groups such as the Center for Immigration Studies. Press coverage has been phenomenal, ranging from articles in small local papers to coverage by major national presses.

Chapter 5 examines various decisions that have been made over the past several years pertaining to undocumented migrants. These include policy proposals at various levels, local laws and ordinances, and various aspects of stepped-up enforcement. Such practices are consistent with what has been labeled an "attrition through enforcement" strategy of addressing undocumented immigration. These are important because in the absence of any practical effects, civilian border groups would remain the disgruntled fringe element I first took them to be in April 2005. The relationship between these immigration "decisions" and civilian border groups should be analyzed with caution, for it is not one of straightforward cause and effect understood in a strict social scientific sense. The decisions made and the exceptions created cannot be attributed solely or directly to border vigilantes. However, the voices of these groups have been very loud (and at times very ugly), and this has contributed significantly to the volume and visibility of the anti-immigrant movement as a whole. The decisions examined in this study are both part and parcel of the anti-immigrant movement as well as consequences that flow from its increasing strength.

Opposition to undocumented immigration has become increasingly well organized and highly vocal, and it has moved from the fringes to the center of the debate. Mark Krikorian of the restrictionist Center for Immigration Studies (CIS) says, "The political center has shifted on this debate, putting CIS right in the middle."[31] The consequences of this shift require that we rethink some of the most important concepts through which we attempt to understand how authority is exercised and how decisions come about that affect the lives of citizens and noncitizens, the documented and the undocumented. Thomas Blom Hansen and Finn Stepputat (2005) have recently suggested that sovereign power and the violence often associated with it should be studied as "practices that are dispersed throughout and across societies." This study is in keeping with that suggestion. In addition, decisions on immigration, and particularly on the undocumented, say a great deal about the core values of a democratic society in an increasingly interconnected world. Harsh policies aimed at human beings who do not have the proper documents to move freely across and within territorial borders reflect the values upon which a society is based. When society becomes structured along the lines of the exception, everyone is ultimately either directly or indirectly affected. As the United Nations' special rapporteur on the human rights of migrants, Jorge A. Bustamante, recently stated, "There is a concern in the United Nations' human rights community about rising anti-immigrant sentiment in the United States."[32] This study contributes to an understanding of this sentiment, how it is sustained and disseminated, and with what consequence.

## 2

## "I'm Proud to Be a Vigilante. How About You?"[1]

### King Anvil Ranch, October 27, 2006

King Anvil Ranch sits on 57,000 acres of desert in Three Points, Arizona, about fifty miles southwest of Tucson. The ranch is at the end of a dirt road about a half-mile off State Route 286. Against a backdrop of the brilliant late-morning sun hanging high over the beautiful (and sacred to the Tohono O'odham) Baboquivari Mountains, we pull onto the dirt road. Directing us to the ranch is a small sign with the words "Welcome Minutemen" and a red arrow under the Minuteman Civil Defense Corps (MCDC) logo, which depicts a revolutionary-era patriot. Another, much larger "Welcome Minutemen" banner is tied to the open gates of the ranch. An American flag is posted on the gate, as well as a smaller sign that says "private property." It is 9:40 a.m. We're scheduled to meet Stacy O'Connell, the MCDC director for the state of Arizona.[2] MCDC volunteer Sandy Doty greets us, signs us in, and gives us each a "Minuteman Civil Defense Corps" temporary identification card. She tells us Stacy will be back at 10 a.m. This is the last week of the MCDC's month-long "Operation Block Watch," which began on September 28 with a kickoff rally attended by several local politicians.[3] In addition to this operation, the MCDC has been stationed on this ranch at various times for the past year and a half.

The King Anvil Ranch has been here since the 1880s, the owners running cattle and raising horses. Back then, Stacy tells us, they had problems with the Cochise Indians—now, it's "illegal aliens." The ranch is thirty-five miles from the U.S.-Mexico border, a one-and-a-half- to two-day walk. Volunteers have come out here from all over the United States for Operation Block Watch. Sandy tells us of Sara Baxter, a seventy-three-year-old lady who came down from Alaska and has been volunteering with the MCDC for the entire month.[4] Another volunteer, who was on an oxygen machine, came from Georgia to participate. They stay in campgrounds on the ranch, in tents and RVs, in motels in town, and in an RV park in town. Why do they come? "Generally speaking, it's because they're tremendously concerned about the safety of our country, the sovereignty of our country," Sandy tells us. Her husband, Quetzal, adds, "And most of them are really concerned about the issue of law. They just feel we have laws on the books and they should be upheld." Quetzal, a retired U.S. diplomatic consular officer, is seventy-two years old.[5] Sandy looks a few years younger. They live in a retirement community on the outskirts of Phoenix, Arizona. Sandy and Quetzal are in charge of registration and background checks. Each volunteer goes through a background check on the Internet, which screens for felony and other criminal convictions. The volunteers pay fifty dollars to cover this expense. I cannot help noting that Sandy and Quetzal and I share the same last name. In our conversation, I discover that we share an ancestor, Edward Doty, who came over on the Mayflower. Sandy tells me of several Web sites for tracing family history.

Stacy O'Connell returns at 10 a.m. with his dog, Migra, a ten-month-old shepherd/husky mix that he picked up a few months ago when MCDC volunteers spotted nineteen migrants walking through the ranch. The Border Patrol took the migrants and Stacy kept the puppy. Stacy looks around forty years old. He's got three kids: one in first grade, one in fourth grade, and a nineteen-year-old. It's not always easy to get out here, he says. His wife supports what he does, though. Stacy got involved in the MCDC during the April 2005 border operation. He says the MCDC is not a bunch of yahoos, but patriots who demand that the rule of law be enforced. Stacy takes us outside to meet Pineapple 6, whose real name is David Jones. Pineapple 6 is an MCDC line boss/section chief. I do not ask how he got the nickname, but wonder if it's because of his shock of extremely thick and wavy white hair, which reminds me of a pineapple. Pineapple 6 is sixty-six years old and, in his own words, a "full-blooded Chocktaw, Delaware Indian."

Shifts for this operation are eight hours long. Volunteers go out from 8 a.m. to 4 p.m., 4 p.m. to midnight, and midnight to 8 a.m. After each shift, the line boss gives the next shift a briefing of any events that occurred during the previous watch, such as the number of "captures," migrant sightings, and so on. Each volunteer goes through a one-hour training session and a one-on-one "vetting," during which the MCDC tries to weed out racists and extremists. It is a bit unclear what this vetting consists of. There is no formal firearms-safety course. "We can only assume that somebody who's gonna carry a sidearm knows how to use it and knows state law," says Stacy. Pineapple 6 tells us that firearms are to stay in the holster unless "your life or your associates' lives is in danger." Only side arms are allowed. No long arms because they look more aggressive.[6] While Stacy and Pineapple are giving the orientation, two MCDC volunteers who have been on patrol for a couple of days are leaving and come to say good-bye. I recognize one as "Maggie's dad," the father of my daughter's school friend.

The "comm ops" (communication operations) room is the "heartbeat of the operation," according to Stacy. It is located inside the house.[7] The room is small and consists of a desk with two manned lines of communication. GPS locators costing eighteen hundred dollars apiece are on every post. The MCDC have three generation-three night-vision cameras with infrared capability, enabling them to see in 100-percent darkness as if it were daylight. They are also equipped with heat-seeking thermal scopes. Even if someone was hiding behind brush, they could be seen. Outside, fifty or so bikes that have been abandoned by migrants in the surrounding desert are stacked against the side of the house. Several pickup trucks and old SUVs are parked in the yard, also abandoned by migrants or their smugglers.

Stacy has agreed to take us to the operation posts. As we head out, following his pickup truck, a call comes in to "comm ops." MCDC volunteers have reported a "sighting" on Route 286. The migrants have scattered, heading down the dirt road leading to the ranch. We pull over. Stacy and Pineapple 6 get out and survey the situation, scouring the ground for footprints. We get out to observe. Novices that we are, not used to hunting other human beings, we do not watch where we step. Pineapple 6 is very concerned and annoyed that we may be stepping on and wiping out the footprints. I'm thinking this would be a good thing. There is a definite feel of "the hunt" in the air, similar to what I felt at the orientation in April 2005. But we don't find anyone, and I breathe a sigh of relief, not wanting to be part of any "capture."

Ike from Atlanta, Georgia and Jim from Branson, Missouri are stationed at Bravo 6. They have been friends since third grade. Jim came to "make a statement." It's been a delight, he says of his time on the ranch. "I think our country's coming into a crisis point." Referring to the migrants, he says, "I have nothing against them. I think they're pretty courageous people." Jim has no objections to a guest worker program. Big problem is with business, he says—Make 'em citizens. It does kind of bother him, though, that the signs along Interstate 19 are posted in kilometers. "I appreciate you being here," he tells me, " 'cause back home they have a misconception of us as redneck, gun-toting vigilantes. We're not. I don't carry a gun. I don't think it's needed." Ike has high regard for migrants as well. They work for him back home, in his lawn service business. He goes down to the corner and picks up however many work-ers he needs. "They're hardworking people. And honorable." This is Ike and Jim's third night patrolling. The first night, twenty to twenty-five migrants came through, says Jim. Ike saw some walking up the road and shone the spotlights on them and they ran. Some had tennis shoes with reflecting soles. Six got left behind and picked up by the Border Patrol.

It is difficult to pigeonhole these people at King Anvil Ranch, as well as others who participate in border watches and anti-immigrant rallies. Based on appearance alone, some would seem to be "walking stereo-types," caricatures of what the term "vigilante" might evoke, like the heavy-set guy from "Americans First" holding up a "No Border. No Or-der" sign and yelling from the back of his pickup truck at an anti-day-labor rally in Phoenix. Or, at the same rally, the guy who referred to himself as "Gandhi in a cowboy hat" and told me that the need for workers in the United States was a direct result of abortions. However, in truth, the picture is more complicated and contradictions abound. Both Ike and Jim were pleasant, soft-spoken guys who conveyed genuine sym-pathy for the plight of undocumented migrants. Ike seemed oblivious to the contradictions entailed in picking up undocumented laborers to work for him paired with the fact that he also patrols the deserts of the southwestern United States trying to capture them. Sandy and Quetzal Doty seemed like long-lost relatives (and they just might be).

At another demonstration at the Mexican Consulate in Phoenix in May 2005, I met Zeffie—the only African American I noticed in the crowd. She had come with her eight-year-old granddaughter. She held two clipboards containing a petition to get an anti-trespassing bill put on the Phoenix ballot as a citizen's initiative. She was anxious to talk and went on and on nonstop, one minute saying how corrupt the govern-ment of Mexico is, the next saying, "But the women and children are pretty good. Am I not right?" or, "We cannot go to their country without papers and you know that is true." Her words at first seemed carefully chosen and spoken very clearly, but after listening to her for a few min-utes, I sensed that it was with great effort that she kept her thoughts focused and her words on track. "What about the women and children?" I asked. "Should they be sent back to Mexico?" "No," she said, "I think they need to be given a chance to stay." Initially confused, it dawned on me that she was getting paid for the signatures she collected. I asked her about this. "One dollar a signature," she said. Raymond, carrying a sign that said "*Viva migra*," described himself as a liberal and said he was not opposed to a guest worker program or the day laborers. He just wanted them off the streets.

Are these people vigilantes? What does a vigilante look like? Of course, there is no definitive answer to this. One cannot escape the controversial nature of this term and the fact that is it generally used in a derogatory sense. However, to think of the groups these people belong to as vigilante groups can also serve a valuable purpose in terms of attempting to understand the phenomenon as a whole. The "everyday people" who attend relatively small and local events make up the larger phenomenon. Without them, the loosely connected "movement" as a whole would not exist. It is in this sense that vigilantism is a useful and I would argue an accurate concept with which to discuss what these groups are all about. This chapter provides a brief background of vigilantism more generally, as well as the ways in which it is specifically enacted on the U.S.-Mexico border. The chapter then examines the various border vigilante groups that have come into existence in the past several years, with a focus on the 2005 Minuteman Project and groups that have formed subsequently.

## Civilian Border Groups as Vigilantes

> We are believers in the doctrine of popular sovereignty; that the people of this country are the real sovereigns, and that whenever the laws, made by those to whom they have delegated their authority, are found inadequate to their protection, it is the right of the people to take the protection of their property into their owns hands . . .[8]
> We can't rely on law enforcement to enforce the laws.
> (Simcox, October 24, 2002)[9]

Vigilantism has a long and varied history in the United States, as well as in many other countries.[10] As the above quote illustrates, it is intimately connected with sovereignty—particularly popular sovereignty—and it entails at least an implicit relationship to the law, and by extension, to the state. Vigilantism is also imbued with controversy. The term and the phenomena it represents are multifaceted and usually emotionally highly charged. Many, though not all, members of the 2005 Minuteman Project and their supporters strenuously objected to President George Bush's reference to them as vigilantes. While there is much variation amongst the different groups examined here, the civilian border phenomenon as a whole shares some interesting features with earlier vigilante groups.

Richard Maxwell Brown (1975: 127) makes the distinction between *classic vigilantism*, which was directed at horse thieves, counterfeiters, outlaws, and "bad men," and *neovigilantism*, which arose after the Civil War and was directed at specific groups such as Catholics, Jews, African Americans, labor leaders, immigrants, and proponents of civil liberties. Immigrants were repeatedly victims of neovigilante attacks, the most spectacular being the lynching of eleven Sicilians in New Orleans in 1891. Laborers and union organizers, many of whom were immigrants, were also victims of this kind of vigilante violence (Brown, 1975: 129). Similarly, Mike Davis (2006: 15–20) differentiates white *southern-style vigilantism*—based on overt racism and entailing obvious and extreme forms of physical violence—from *western-style vigilantism*—which justified itself in the name of upholding unenforced laws. This latter form of vigilantism can be traced to romanticized notions of frontier democracy and justice and the founding of the United States.[11] More recent instances of vigilante movements, specifically in the 1960s and early 1970s, differed from classic or southern-style vigilantism in that their main activities consisted of patrol actions for the purpose of spotting and reporting. This often entailed cooperation with the local police, resulting in something of a parallel structure of law enforcement.

Many similarities exist between the sentiments of members of contemporary civilian border groups and earlier vigilante groups. This is quite evident in Jim Gilchrist's recent remarks as he stood before Daniel Chester French's original Minuteman statue in Concord, Massachusetts on the site where white colonists battled British troops on April 19, 1776 and sounded the shot that marked the start of the American Revolution. "I feel connected," Gilchrist said. "What they created stays with us 230 years later—I would hope. A nation governed under the rule of law, and not at the whim of the mob—of tens of millions of illegal aliens."[12] The themes that resonate throughout the slogans and calls to action on the part of contemporary border vigilantes focus on law and order, security, and the inadequacy of official realms of the law and law enforcement. Various aspects of the social order are presumed to be under threat and these groups are reacting to this perceived threat. First, there is the physical border itself. In his study of the vigilante tradition in the United States, Brown (1975: 96–99) suggests that vigilantism arose as a response to the absence of effective law and order in frontier regions where regular systems of law enforcement were often inadequate. As pioneers in the United States moved west across the Appalachian Mountains, the vigilante impulse followed and became a model for dealing with frontier disorder. Vigilante groups viewed outlaws and those who were either marginal or alienated from the community as desirous of upsetting the existing social structure and thus a threat.[13] Not surprisingly, the frontier is also a prominent theme with contemporary border vigilantes. Groups such as the Minuteman Project, the Minuteman Civil Defense Corps, American Border Patrol, Ranch Rescue, and others draw even more fundamentally on the frontier element in that it is not simply disorder on the frontier that motivates them, but the very integrity of the frontier itself *as* frontier. The territorial line that separates Mexico from the United States figures prominently. Territorial borders are powerful symbols of sovereignty and the specter of *la linea* out of control is a powerful symbol for these groups that enables their cause to resonate with broader audiences. The actions that have been most widely publicized by the media, as well as on the groups' own Web sites, have had to do with the physical patrolling of the U.S.-Mexico border regions in addition to the highlighting of various grievances of those who live in close proximity to the border, such as ranchers and other property owners.[14]

However, the notion of the frontier as physical border should not be understood too narrowly or too literally. While the territorial frontier is a powerful symbol, border vigilante groups are about much more than the physical border. Many of those involved in border vigilante groups are not from border communities and until fairly recently had little experience with the various aspects of life in border regions. Chris Simcox moved to Tombstone from California. Ditto for Glenn Spencer. Jim Gilchrist lives in California. Indeed, one of the criticisms of the Minuteman Project in the spring of 2005 was that it consisted mainly of people from outside the region and thus of people with little understanding of the complex relationship between towns on the Mexican side of the border and those on the U.S. side. Still, the notion of the contemporary border vigilante phenomenon being a frontier phenomenon is appropriate if we maintain a broad conceptualization of the frontier. As the number of undocumented migrants working and living in many communities across the United States continues to rise, "the border" comes to mean much more than the physical markers that separate the two countries. Peter Nyers (2006: 4) suggests that "the border is less of a 'line' across a specific piece of territory than a complex network that is projected both far beyond and well within the territorial space of the state." Such a broadened understanding of the border more readily facilitates making connections between contemporary vigilantism, the broader anti-immigrant movement, and other societal actors.

Vigilante groups draw upon many symbolic borders that are generally framed in hierarchical and oppositional terms, such as the lines between criminality versus law-abiding citizens, invaders versus those who legally belong, the assimilated versus the unassimilated. Criminality has historically been a prominent theme with vigilante groups and continues as a strong element with contemporary border vigilantes. Indeed, it is arguably key to any legitimacy these groups possess. Ray Abrahams (1998) suggests that one aspect of the power of vigilantism to generate ambivalence is the notion of decent, law-abiding citizens, who want to live in peace, defending their right to do so if the state fails them. In this sense, vigilante groups do not reject the state per se but rather seek to supplement it. Indeed, they may actually thrive on the legitimacy of "the state" as an entity of authority, even though they protest the action (or lack of action) on the part of a particular state. The failure of the state to adequately protect its citizens from criminal elements of various stripes gives rise to citizen action to do it themselves, whether by taking the law into their own hands or by engaging in practices that call attention to the failure of the state to do the same.

A focus on the presumed criminality of undocumented migrants who have "invaded" the United States is clearly evident in the rhetoric of contemporary border vigilante groups. Chris Simcox, Stacy O'Connell, and others have described the MCDC as a "neighborhood watch group," drawing upon the notion of citizens vigilantly patrolling their neighborhoods, protecting themselves and their families from criminal activity.[15] Other examples abound. Two typical ones include American Patrol's call for supporters to "Rally Against Invader Amnesty" and their referencing of an article from San Diego's KNSD-TV—whose original headline read, "Rescuers Free People Trapped in Border Storm Drain," but which was altered on American Patrol's home page to read, "Invaders 'rescued' from cross-border tunnel."[16] Another example can be found on the Web site of Mothers Against Illegal Aliens: "Our beautiful Nation has been turned into a jungle by the mass invasion of illegal aliens."[17] Human beings become "invaders," and by implication, enemies. The criminality theme is obviously present in demands for stronger border enforcement, but also underpins the vociferous opposition to any kind of "amnesty" or guest worker program. The very term amnesty implies a wrongdoing; thus, this label itself is rife with negative connotations. When I asked Minuteman Grey Deacon what he thought of a guest worker program, he said, "Why do we need a guest worker program? Do we have a guest murderer program?"[18] Jim Gilchrist and others repeatedly equate undocumented migrants with criminality. Gilchrist says that "The U.S. is engaged in a 'silent war' conducted by illegal aliens that is causing a higher toll than the war in Iraq," claiming that more U.S. citizens have been "killed in action" by undocumented migrants than soldiers have been killed in Iraq.[19] This claim is often repeated in other anti-immigrant forums.[20] This stereotype is old and to some has come to be considered conventional wisdom. However, it lacks empirical foundation. A recent study published by the Migration Policy Institute highlights the fact that connections between immigration and crime have rarely been carefully researched using rigorous evidence.[21]

## Vigilant Citizens on the U.S.-Mexico Border

The April 2005 Minuteman Project was by no means the first instance of private citizens taking it upon themselves to patrol the U.S.-Mexico border. In August of 1976, three Mexican nationals—Manuel Garcia Loya, Eleazar Ruelas Zavala, and Bernabe Herrera Mata—crossed into the United States in Cochise County, Arizona, without legal authorization. Rancher George Hanigan and his two sons, Patrick and Thomas, approached the three men in their pickup truck as they drank water just west of Highway 80. The Hanigans forced the men into the camper of their truck and drove to Highway 80, then west onto their ranch, where they tied the hands and ankles of Manuel, Eleazar, and Bernabe. They robbed them, sliced their clothes off with a knife, and took turns dragging them with ropes near a fire the brothers had started, then proceeding to burn their clothes. The Hanigans subsequently released the three men, firing shots at them as they ran south toward the Mexican border.[22]

In October of 1977, Grand Dragon Tom Metzger and Imperial Wizard David Duke organized the Klan Border Watch at the San Ysidro, California, port of entry.[23] Metzger, a San Diego television repairman, was also engaged in other anti-immigrant, anti-Mexican demonstrations in the San Diego area.[24] Three years after the Klan Border Watch, Metzger ran for Congress in California, campaigning openly as a Klansman and promising that he would militarize the border.[25] In 1986, the *New York Times* reported that members of an anti-communist paramilitary group, Civilian Materiel Assistance, had captured fifteen undocumented migrants on the Arizona-Mexico border. The incident took place in the Lochiel Valley, three miles north of the Mexican border and about thirty miles east of Nogales, Arizona.[26] These incidents, though quite serious, were relatively isolated and it was not until the late 1980s and early 1990s that civilian border patrol groups began to attract "ordinary" citizens as well as the attention of the media. At this time, the majority operated along the U.S.-Mexico border in the San Diego area.

In 1989, an ad-hoc collection of citizens in twenty-three cars gathered along a road overlooking the San Diego-Tijuana border and beamed their headlights on the area in an effort at "passive deterrence" aimed at those trying to cross the border under the cover of darkness. The group, which became known as "Light Up The Border," was started by Muriel Watson, the widow of a U.S. Border Patrol agent who wanted the federal government to install lights and a fence along the border. This kind of "light-up" protest was repeated many times over the next year and in March 1990 more than one thousand people parked their cars and shone headlights toward Tijuana. Encouraged by former San Diego mayor and local radio station KOGO talk-show host Roger Hedgecock, an equal number of people turned out again in April and slightly fewer in May.[27] The Light Up The Border movement soon faded, but San Diego resident Ben Seeley went on to found the Border Solution Task Force. Other groups formed, and what might be called an informal, loosely connected citizens' anti-immigrant movement began to grow. This movement revolves around the notion of societal security discussed in the previous chapter. The underlying themes voiced by members of the various groups that make up the movement focus on concerns with the presumed threats posed by migrants to the identity and survival of the United States. They demonstrate that articulations of security concerns do not necessarily come primarily from the state or government actors. The very existence of these groups and the practices they engage in are pronouncements of popular sovereignty, reminding leaders that "the people" are the true source of sovereignty.

In 1992, Glenn Spencer, then a resident of California, founded a neighborhood group in response to the race riots that broke out in Los Angeles that year after the beating of Rodney King by Los Angeles Police Department officers. Referring to images of Latinos plundering the Hollywood Sears store, Spencer said, "I was stunned and thought, 'Oh, my God, there are so many of them and they are so out of control.' "[28] He named his group Valley Citizens Together, subsequently renaming it Voices of Citizens Together as he linked poverty, violence, and other social problems in Los Angeles to undocumented immigration. Voices of Citizens Together was active in California's Save our State movement, a loose coalition of anti-immigrant groups who advocated mass deportation of undocumented immigrants. The movement culminated in the passage of California's anti-immigrant Proposition 187 in 1994.[29]

In 1994, work began on a fourteen-mile fence along the flat grassland of Otay Mesa, east of the port of entry at San Ysidro.[30] When the fence was still not completed by 1997, Glenn Spencer staged a "Good Fences Make Good Neighbors" demonstration at the border. Speaking at the demonstration, San Diego County Supervisor Diane Jacob said, "There's a crime that has been committed. Our government has failed to enforce our borders, failed to protect the lives and property of the United States citizens, and has ripped off U.S. taxpayers."[31] Spencer has since become one of the leading voices in the anti-immigrant movement. The Southern Poverty Law Center, a nonprofit organization that tracks hate groups and hate crimes, refers to him as "a Paul Revere of the anti-immigrant movement."[32]

In September 2002, Spencer moved to the southeastern Arizona community of Sierra Vista and set up his new organization, American Border Patrol. "California is a lawless, lost state," Spencer is quoted as saying. "It's a mess. There's nothing I can do for California. It is finished."[33] He recruited two former U.S. Border Patrol agents to join his new organization and held public meetings to explain the goals of the group, which was incorporated in Arizona in 2002.[34] With the help of citizen volunteers, Spencer conducts surveillance missions near the border. The volunteers position themselves near ground sensors. When the sensors are triggered by migrants, volunteer teams move into position and record the migrants on video cameras. The videos are shown on American Border Patrol's Web site. With permission from the U.S. Federal Aviation Administration, Spencer's group also conducts surveillance missions along the U.S.-Mexico border using unmanned aerial vehicles equipped with cameras and GPS technology.[35] The group's Web site contains links to numerous other organizations, as well as a link to the U.S.

Border Patrol, with phone numbers for reporting undocumented immigrants.[36] The Southern Poverty Law Center added American Border Patrol to their list of hate groups in the fall of 2001.[37] According to the Anti-Defamation League, Spencer blends "anti-Mexican bigotry with anti-government rhetoric in order to tap into deeply embedded fears and to encourage citizens to take the law into their own hands."[38]

Spencer has long been a proponent of *reconquista theory*, a notion that there is a plot on the part of Mexico to retake the southwestern United States. He believes that Mexico has declared war on the United States: "The United States is being invaded by Mexico. Mexican gangs roam our streets. Mexican drugs destroy our children. Mexican politicians threaten White Americans with extinction."[39] Spencer refers to the time we are living in as "pre-war America," stating: "There is going to be a civil war of a kind we've never seen before, because the government hasn't allowed the problem to work itself out in the public arena."[40] In 2004, Spencer was sentenced to one year of probation and fined $2,500 for recklessly firing a gun.[41] The same year, the property association where he lived evicted him for running a business out of his home and he moved his operations to Palominas, Arizona.

American Border Patrol's Web site references the Web site of fellow civilian border patrol group Ranch Rescue.[42] In reciprocity, Ranch Rescue lists American Border Patrol on its links page. Prior to the 2005 Minuteman Project, Ranch Rescue was probably the most publicized of the civilian border patrol groups. Ranch Rescue originated in Arlington, Texas, in 2000. This group was formed by Jack Foote and a small group of people who were inspired by stories of rancher Roger Barnett, who lives on a 22,000-acre ranch two miles north of the border near Douglas, Arizona. Barnett actively seeks out undocumented migrants trespassing on his land, sometimes tracking them for miles. When he catches them, he holds them for the U.S. Border Patrol. He has been accused of threatening them with weapons and has been investigated by Cochise County and federal officials.[43] Barnett told *Time Magazine* writer Tim McGirk Douglas of a specific incident:

> One fellow tried to get up and walk away, saying we're not Immigration. So I slammed him back down and took his photo. 'Why'd you do that?' the illegal says, all surprised. 'Because we want you to go home with a before picture and an after picture—that is, after we beat the s— outta you.' You can bet he started behavin' then.[44]

Barnett claims to have made citizen's arrests of more than twelve thousand undocumented migrants since 1996.[45] The Center for Human Rights and the Constitutional Law Foundation report that it is widely believed that the Barnett family is well connected to local law enforcement.[46] In November 2006, Barnett was found guilty in a civil trial in Superior Court in Bisbee, Arizona, of intentionally inflicting emotional distress and committing negligence and unlawful imprisonment, and he was ordered to pay $98,750 in damages to two Mexican-American hunters and their three children. Currently pending in federal court is another case in which Barnett, along with his brother and wife, is accused of pointing guns at sixteen undocumented migrants they intercepted, threatening them with dogs, and kicking one woman in the group.[47]

Ranch Rescue conducted their first "operation" in Douglas, Arizona, in 2000 ostensibly to help ranchers repair property damage that resulted from undocumented migrants crossing on their lands.[48] The following year, they undertook Operation Hawk, and their latest undertaking was Operation Eagle on the Arizona border in the fall of 2005. During operations like these, members deck themselves out in military-style garb, armed with 5.56-millimeter assault rifles and .45-caliber pistols, as well as AKs, SKSs, and 9-millimeter/.30-caliber Tokarev arms.[49] The group's Web site quotes a section from Jean Raspail's anti-immigrant novel *The Camp of the Saints*: "You don't know my people—the squalor, the superstitions, the fatalistic sloth that they've wallowed in for generations. You don't know what you're in for if that fleet of brutes ever lands in your lap."

Ranch Rescue's Web site provides an "Affiliate Membership Form," which requests that members "certify and affirm that there is no USA state or federal laws that prohibit me from purchasing, owning, or possessing firearms."[50] The group received a great deal of attention in October 2002 when members of one of their armed patrols seized 280 pounds of marijuana from smugglers crossing a ranch in Lochiel, Arizona. They received more attention in March 2003 when, during Operation Falcon in Hebbronville, Texas, two volunteers were arrested for detaining two Salvadorans and beating one with a pistol. The Ranch Rescue volunteers were charged with aggravated assault and unlawful restraint.[51] Fatima Leiva and Edwin Mancia were detained by Ranch Rescue member James Casey Nethercott. During their detention, Nethercott struck Mancia on the back of the head and allowed his rottweiler to attack him.[52] It has been reported that as a result of the lawsuit stemming from this incident, Ranch Rescue and its leaders have been forced to declare bankruptcy.[53]

According to Chris Simcox of the MCDC, Ranch Rescue no longer exists. When asked if his group had any connection to Ranch Rescue, Simcox said, "Ranch Rescue does not exist. It never existed other than about a handful of people."[54] However, the group's Web site indicates that they are still in existence and solicits funds for a group called Border Rescue, of which Jack Foote was the spokesman until 2004. It is unclear what the organization's current status is or if it is now actively involved in border operations.[55]

## D-Day, Tombstone, Arizona, April 1, 2005[56]

> Stand your ground! Don't fire unless fired upon, but if they mean to have a war, let it begin here.[57]

Chris Simcox started the Tombstone Militia after a two-and-a-half-month-long "camping" session in the Arizona desert following the September 11, 2001 attacks.[58] Simcox, a former kindergarten teacher at Wildwood, a private school in Los Angeles, lost his job and family after 9/11. "Everything crumbled," he said. "From 9/11 to Oct. 1, my entire life fell apart, I lost my clients, I lost custody of my son . . . I just chucked it all and left."[59] Simcox moved to Tombstone, Arizona, and spent several weeks hiking, camping, and tracking a group conducting smuggling operations near Organ Pipe National Monument. He hid in the bush and tracked them for three weeks. He says he was "scared for [his] life." He then spent the next month making his way east along the Arizona border to Nogales. His desert odyssey convinced Simcox that he needed to do something to prevent the "invasion" he had witnessed. He tried to join the Border Patrol, but at forty-one he was too old. He arrived in Tombstone in November 2001, went to work as a reporter for the *Tombstone Tumbleweed*, and began going out on patrol, sometimes alone, sometimes with a small group of friends. He became convinced that undocumented immigration is a national security issue and that it is up to the citizenry to do what the government has failed to do. When *the Tombstone Tumbleweed* came up for sale in May 2002, Simcox bought it.[60]

In October 2002, Simcox used the paper to launch a "call to arms" and formed the Tombstone Militia. He said:

> Yes, we are a Militia and we intend to be a part of the organized armed forces of a country liable to call only in emergency. We have the right

to organize. We actually have more freedom to tackle the problem than the Government and law enforcement agencies that are bogged down in the quagmire of laws and restrictions. (Simcox, October 31, 2002)

In a statement to the *Washington Times*, Simcox said:

I dare the president of the United States to arrest Americans who are protecting their own country. We will no longer tolerate the ineptness of the government in dealing with these criminals and drug dealers. It is a monumental disgrace that our government is letting the American people down, turning us into the expendable casualties of the war on terrorism.[61]

In January 2003, Simcox was arrested by federal park rangers in Arizona while hunting for undocumented immigrants with a loaded pistol, a digital camera, walkie-talkies, and paramilitary gear. It is illegal to carry firearms in the Coronado National Forest, where he was arrested. In May 2004, he was convicted of carrying a concealed weapon on federal land and lying to a federal officer about it and was sentenced to two years of probation.[62] Simcox attracted the attention of white nationalist columnist Sam Francis, who echoed his sentiments, writing: "If the government won't enforce the law, the citizens whom the law is supposed to protect and from whom the law ultimately derives must do it themselves" (Francis, 2002).

In March 2003, Simcox wrote in an e-mail: "Do not attempt to cross the border illegally; you will be considered an enemy of the state; if aggressors attempt to forcefully enter our country they will be repelled with force if necessary!"[63]

Simcox changed the name of his organization to Civil Homeland Defense. The fall of 2004 marked a turning point when he spoke on George Putnam's KCAA AM 1050 conservative talk radio program in California. Jim Gilchrist, a Vietnam vet and retired accountant, heard him. After the broadcast, Gilchrist called Simcox and offered to help him organize volunteer civilian border patrols. "Things came out that were in my head swimming around for years," Gilchrist said. "It was a culmination of fears building up."[64] The Minuteman Project was born and recruitment began. Gilchrist made use of the Internet, targeting his appeals to veterans, ex-Border Patrol agents, and others, calling on them to serve their country. Beginning on April 1, 2005 with much media fanfare, the

Minuteman Project officially began. Volunteers were "screened" at the project's headquarters, the *Tombstone Tumbleweed* office, and Simcox and other project leaders conducted orientation sessions at the Palominas Trading Post. Operations were set up along Border Road in Naco, Arizona, and along Highway 92 in Palominos, Arizona. Citizen volunteers manned posts around the clock, watching for undocumented migrants. The American Civil Liberties Union sent legal observers to watch the volunteers.

On April 18, 2005, Jim Gilchrist announced that "because of the phenomenal success of this grassroots project in such a short time, the Minuteman Project has declared an unconditional victory in its efforts." Gilchrist said, "We will be taking our message to the Congressional Immigration Reform Caucus at the invitation of its chair, Congressman Tom Tancredo (R-CO)."[65] On the same day, Simcox announced that the Civil Homeland Defense volunteers would "assume full operational control of the civilian border-watch effort through the end of the month and will continue the effort indefinitely."[66]

Jim Gilchrist continues to head the Minuteman Project while Chris Simcox heads the Minuteman Civil Defense Corps. Bob Wright, an organizer for the Minuteman Project, said that the project was just a "beachhead for a nationwide effort to secure this nation's borders."[67] Almost immediately after its formation, stories of the "success" of the Minuteman Project became accepted as truth. Gilchrist and Simcox became "experts" on immigration and their views were sought by the media and policy makers. The following excerpt is illustrative: "After demonstrating in Arizona that a presence of people along the border can cut illegal immigration, border control proponents came to Washington to try to win over the minds and money of the federal government." The article in which this quote appears is referring to a meeting between Gilchrist, Simcox, and the Congressional Immigration Reform Caucus (CIRC).[68] The CIRC was founded in 1999 by conservative Colorado congressman Tom Tancredo. It promotes restrictionist immigration policies and since 9/11 has increasingly linked immigration with terrorism.[69]

## Beyond April 2005

Tom Tancredo refers to the April 2005 Minuteman Project as "a watershed event that changed the immigration reform debate forever."[70] It has become a powerful symbol and a rallying point for those who advocate stronger immigration enforcement along the U.S.-Mexico border, but also internally.[71] Both Simcox's Minuteman Civil Defense Corps and Gilchrist's Minuteman Project (MMP) have continued various anti-immigrant operations both at the U.S.-Mexico border and in cities throughout the United States. During the months of November and December 2005, the Minuteman Civil Defense Corps began a campaign to prevent the hiring of day laborers who gather at various locations throughout U.S. cities hoping for work. In Phoenix, Arizona, they chose the corner of Thirty-sixth Street and Thomas, a location that generally has a large number of day laborers waiting for work. Every Saturday morning from 8 a.m. until 11 a.m., members of the Minuteman Civil Defense Corps and their supporters gathered with a display of anti-immigrant slogans. Participants were told to bring cameras and video equipment and tape contractors that picked up workers. On December 10, Chris Simcox showed up and was flanked by local reporters as well as reporters from the *Washington Post* and a French TV station. The campaign took place in several cities throughout the United States, including Herndon, Virginia, Redondo Beach and Laguna, California, and Brewster, New York.[72]

In May 2006, Minuteman Project leaders embarked on a cross-country caravan beginning in Los Angeles and ending in Washington, D.C. The purpose of the tour was to gather support for tighter border controls, and it was in part a counter to the massive immigrant rights marches on April 10, 2006. On May 4, the caravan came through Phoenix, Arizona, and a group of supporters gathered at the State Capitol to welcome them. Local reporters surrounded Jim Gilchrist and supporters waved large American flags and signs. One prominent sign read, "We Don't Want Your Stinko De Mayo," presumably referring to Cinco De Mayo. Another sign displayed in big, bold black letters: "TAKE AN ILLEGAL ALIEN DOWN." In much smaller print at the bottom of the sign were the words, "To The Border (and send them home.)"[73] Pamela and Clayton of Apache Junction, Arizona, each held flagpoles attached to large U.S. flags. They said they were members of the Minuteman Project, but had not yet participated in any of its border operations. When I asked if they thought mass deportation was a solution, Clayton replied, "If I robbed a bank ten years ago, should I get off?"[74] I presumed this was a "yes" on the deportation question.

On September 11, 2006, the Minuteman Project launched "Operation Sovereignty," which was scheduled to run through November 7, Election

Day. Jim Gilchrist teamed up with the Minuteman Project's Texas branch and with Glenn Spencer's American Border Patrol to track undocumented migrants and report them to the U.S. Border Patrol.[75] Gilchrist has attempted to distance himself and the Minuteman Project, at least rhetorically, from the more openly racist elements that are often attracted to the anti-immigrant movement. Their Web site states: "The Minuteman Project has no affiliation with, nor will we accept any assistance by or interference from separatists, racists or supremacy groups or individuals, no matter what their race, color, or creed."[76] Yet Gilchrist adheres to the same belief in the "reconquista conspiracy" as one finds in the American Border Patrol, saying, "From what I have seen in videos, to me there is a clear and present danger of insurrection, sedition and succession by those who buy into the fact that this really is Mexico's territory and doesn't belong to the United States and should be taken back."[77]

In the spring of 2006, both the MMP and the MCDC launched separate multi-state civilian border patrol operations. Gilchrist said, "I'm willing to see my country go to battle if necessary for our sovereignty and to be governed by rule of law."[78] Simcox took a less inflammatory stance, which is consistent with what some call the "new Simcox, groomed and scripted by neoconservative political consultants."[79] An increasing portion of Simcox's time is spent at forums and fundraising. Early in 2006, he was a featured panelist at the Conservative Political Action Conference in Washington, D.C., the nation's largest gathering of conservative political activists.[80]

In addition to Simcox's and Gilchrist's groups, numerous other citizen border watch groups have formed across the country. By the fall of 2005, the Southern Poverty Law Center reported that more than forty anti-immigrant citizen border patrol groups had formed since April 2005, many of them far from the actual U.S-Mexico border.[81] By the spring of 2007, this number had climbed to 144, 57 of the groups being chapters of either Simcox's Minuteman Civil Defense Corps or Gilchrist's Minuteman Project.[82] The other groups are independent, and some are openly disowned by Gilchrist and Simcox. Heidi Beirich, deputy director of the Southern Poverty Law Center, says that the anti-immigrant movement is exploding with the development of more and more new organizations in addition to new chapters of existing organizations.[83] Financial contributions to these groups have also increased. Glenn Spencer's group reports a 25-percent increase in donations.[84]

One of the groups to form after April 2005 is the California Minutemen, also referred to as California Border Watch and United States Border Patrol Auxiliary. This group was founded by James Chase, who was a prominent member of the original Minuteman Project in Arizona. Chase announced that, unlike Gilchrist and Simcox—who had at least articulated a handguns-only policy—his recruits would be allowed to carry hunting rifles, assault rifles, and shotguns. He also encouraged them to bring baseball bats, stun guns, and machetes.[85] While Chris Simcox distances himself from the California Minutemen, Jim Gilchrist was present to show his support when they launched their first operation in the California border town of Campo.[86] On July 18, 2005, Gilchrist put out a call for reinforcements in Campo.[87] In September 2005, American Border Patrol and the Friends of the Border Patrol joined the California Minuteman in a border vigil.[88]

Another group, the Border Guardians, are a new anti-immigrant, vigilante group led by Laine Lawless. While not formally connected to either Simcox's Minuteman Civil Defense Corps or Gilchrist's Minuteman Project, the Border Guardians were clearly inspired by these two groups, displaying an article on their Web site entitled: "How the Minuteman Project Changed Everything."[89] Laine Lawless was an original member of Chris Simcox's Civil Homeland Defense before it became the Minuteman Civil Defense Corps.[90] The mission of the Border Guardians is to "disrupt and deter illegal immigration by any legal means, including psy-ops field missions, propaganda, and infiltration of organizations who are enemies of the lawful American republic and American citizenry as a whole."[91] Their Web site advertises T-shirts with the words "PROUD NATIVIST AMERICAN—Defending American Sovereignty" on the fronts.

The group received national and international media attention in April 2006 when members engaged in Mexican flag-burning ceremonies in Tucson, Arizona. On April 9, Lawless and Tucson anti-immigrant activists Russell Dove and Roy Warden burned a Mexican flag in front of the Mexican consulate in Tucson. On April 10, the day of nationwide immigrant rights marches and rallies, Lawless, Dove, and Warden burned two more Mexican flags. Warden shouted, "And if any invader tries to take this land from us, we will wash this land with blood."[92] The idea of burning Mexican flags originated with nationally syndicated conservative talk radio host Michael Savage, based in San Francisco. On March 27, Savage had called upon his listeners to "burn a Mexican flag for America, burn a Mexican flag for those who died that you should have a nationality and a sovereignty, go out in the street and show you're a man, burn ten Mexican flags, if I could recommend it."[93]

Roy Warden said, "We are engaged in a great civil war."[94] Around the same time, the Southern Poverty Law Center obtained a copy of an e-mail sent to neo-Nazi group the National Socialist Movement, which has fifty-nine chapters in thirty states. The e-mail was from Laine Lawless and was entitled "How to GET RID OF THEM." It contains a list of several tactics, "some legal and some not-so." Lawless states in the text, "I'm not ready to come out on this, but I think my ideas are good and should be shared." And: "Maybe some of your warriors for the race would be the kind of ppl' [sic] willing to implement some of these ideas. Please don't use my name."[95] The list of tactics included: "Steal the money from any illegal walking into a bank or check cashing place," "Create an anonymous propaganda campaign warning that any further illegal immigrants coming here will be shot, maimed, or seriously messed up crossing the border," and, "Discourage Spanish-speaking school children from going to public school. Be creative."[96]

The group got attention when a Phoenix TV reporter for the local CBS station, KPHO, went undercover with a hidden camera and caught Lawless admitting she'd accept racists into the group.[97] The group received additional attention in May 2006 when Roy Warden sent an e-mail to Isabel Garcia of Derechos Humanos, a migrant rights group in Tucson, Arizona, saying, "I will not hesitate to draw my weapon and blow your freaking heads off."[98] The Border Guardians hosted another Mexican flag-burning ceremony on December 16, 2006, in front of the Mexican Consulate in Phoenix, after which Laine Lawless attended the neo-Nazi National Vanguard's Winterfest in Phoenix.[99] Participating in this event was Donald Pauly of the Emigration Party of Nevada who, according to the Southern Poverty Law Center, is one of the most abrasive figures in the anti-immigrant movement.[100]

The group Mothers Against Illegal Aliens (MAIA), which has strong connections with Gilchrist and the Minuteman Project, rallied with the Border Guardians on February 18 to 20, 2006, in Hereford, Arizona. The Border Guardians also invited the public to attend the rally in support of Mothers Against Illegal Aliens. MAIA was started by Phoenix resident Michelle Dallacroce, who has connections both to Gilchrist's Minuteman Project and Simcox's Minuteman Civil Defense Corps. She was a visible and vocal presence at the November/December 2005 anti-day-labor demonstrations organized by Simcox's group. She has also traveled to Washington, D.C. with Gilchrist and she spoke at the Minuteman Caravan's stop in Phoenix. MAIA's Web site displays Dallacroce's photo with Tom Tancredo and Bay Buchanan (Pat Buchanan's sister), along with the following text underneath the photo:

> Our beautiful Nation has been turned into a jungle by the mass invasion of illegal aliens—the streets of America; the neighborhoods and communities where we live; the malls and stores where we shop; the schools where our LEGAL children attend—and yes, even the churches where we worship—are now Citadels of fear, bigotry, racism, physical danger and hate.[101]

The most recent project of Mothers Against Illegal Aliens involved a trip to Chicago by Dallacroce and Carmen Mercer, vice president of the Minuteman Civil Defense Corps, to protest against Elvira Arellano, the woman who was given refuge in the Adalberto Methodist Church in Chicago's Humboldt Park.[102]

Michelle Dallacroce spoke at a rally at the Mexican Consulate in Phoenix in May 2005. The rally was announced on American Patrol's Web site and was sponsored by "Americans First, A Pro-American, Pro-Secure Borders, Pro-Sovereignty, Pro-LEGAL and Humane Immigration Group."[103] One of Dallacroce's favorite issues is the birthright citizenship of babies born in the United States to parents who are undocumented. Dallacroce plays upon motherhood and the duty to protect children. She has a somewhat narrow definition, though, of who deserves protection—specifically, "LEGAL children," a category that in her mind excludes those referred to in a derogatory way as "anchor babies." "The LEGAL children of America's 21st century," she says, "have become the scapegoats and the victims of this invasion of illegal aliens."[104] MAIA claims that illegal migrants bring diseases like tuberculosis and leprosy into the country and endanger U.S. children.[105] For Dallacroce and her group, "the enemy" includes the children of undocumented migrants, regardless of the fact that they are U.S. citizens. Clearly, she is calling for making exceptions to the Fourteenth Amendment of the U.S. Constitution, which guarantees birthright citizenship. "You fix the 14th Amendment, you have fixed 3/4 of the problems and costs associated with illegal immigration."[106]

The rally at the Mexican Consulate was attended by approximately one hundred anti-immigrant protesters, as well as a small group of about thirty from the Phoenix Anarchist Coalition, who rallied in support of migrants and against those from Americans First. Lee Greenwood's country and western music hit "God Bless the U.S.A." played loudly throughout the entire afternoon, drowning out the rap music on the boom box of the pro-immigrant anarchists. "We hate the illegals, our border should be closed," said Louise Lonsdale of Phoenix.[107] Participants waved signs displaying the words "Invaders Go Home," "No Amnesty. Seal Our Borders Now," and an assortment of other slogans that have become somewhat commonplace. I spoke with several people at this rally and received written feedback from some.[108] One young man, aged thirty-three, who identified his race as "Aryan," commented that "if our republic does not get a grip on massive illegal immigration, we will lose our form of government, lose our middle class, and whites will be slaughtered in a bloody revolution one day."

Clearly, there is much hyperbole, extremism, and "over-the-top" characters that are part of border vigilante groups. This makes for colorful and sometimes entertaining, sometimes disturbing stories, but the real importance is to be found in the themes and sentiments that resonate with larger audiences and that function to sustain and legitimate these groups. Evident in these themes and sentiments is the notion of an enemy. This is more obvious in some instances—such as the Mexican flag-burning activities of groups like the Border Guardians—than in others, but it is also clearly evident in calls telling migrants to "go home," or designating them as "invaders." The construction of undocumented migrants as enemies is widespread and often more subtle than the shouts of vigilantes protesting on city streets or at our southern border. Groups discussed in this chapter are connected in both direct and indirect ways to other organizations and elements within society. In the following chapter, I examine the connections between border vigilantes and the broader anti-immigrant movement, as well as connections between these groups and white nationalists/supremacists, groups whose focus is national security, and Christian right groups.

# 3

# "It's Your Country, Take it Back."[1]

Representative Tom Tancredo looks into the audience and asks members of the April 2005 Minuteman Project to stand up. About fifteen people stand. He then fixes his gaze upon Jim Gilchrist, who is also in the audience, and says, "I see the champion of that endeavor," adding, "I love to be able to call myself a Minuteman." A round of enthusiastic applause follows. The occasion is the Southwest Conference on Illegal Immigration, Border Security, and Crime in Scottsdale, Arizona, hosted by Maricopa Country attorney Andrew Thomas in November 2005.[2] A group called Veterans for Secure Borders has posted a large sign at the entrance to the conference with the words, "Mr. President, Sir: They Didn't Die for Open Borders." Frank Gaffney, president of the Center for Security Policy, is equipped with a stack of fliers displaying the words "War Footing" in large red letters and underneath, "10 steps America Must Take to Prevail in the War for the Free World." The first step is "know the enemy." The seventh is "secure our borders and interior against illegal immigration." Gaffney refers to "the Arizona front in the war for the free world."[3] Another group, protectAZborder.com, passes out a booklet entitled "Common Sense on Mass Immigration," published by the Social Contract Press. While some of the invited guests represent moderate or pro-immigrant points of view, such as Representative Ben Miranda of the Arizona House of Representatives, Eleanor Eisenberg—former executive director of the Arizona American Civil Liberties Union (ACLU)—and attorney Daniel Ortega, for the most part, the roster of speakers reads like a "who's who" list of the national anti-immigrant movement.

On Saturday morning's first panel, Arizona senator J.D. Hayworth had proclaimed that "we are a nation at war." Rick Oltman, at the time the western regional field representative for the Federation for American Immigration Reform, referred to the Minuteman Project as one of the events that changed the landscape in discussions on immigration reform. Tancredo, the closing speaker, began his remarks by saying, "This is where the battle lines are drawn."

This conference was just one of several that followed on the heels of the April 2005 Minuteman border operations. On May 29, 2005, several anti-immigrant groups held a conference in Las Vegas to praise the Minutemen's April operations and to call for stronger border enforcement. The conference, "Unite to Fight Against Illegal Immigration," was sponsored by the Las Vegas-based Wake Up America Foundation, which is chaired by Las Vegas talk radio host Mark Edwards.[4] At that conference, too, the keynote speaker was Tom Tancredo. Other speakers included Jim Gilchrist, Chris Simcox, Glenn Spencer of American Border Patrol, Rick Oltman of the Federation for American Immigration Reform, and John Vinson of American Immigration Control Foundation.[5] Chris Simcox told the attendees that his group of fifteen thousand was committed to defending the nation's borders: "We want the border secured. Nothing less will be accepted. There is no compromise."[6] In response to demonstrators protesting the conference, some of whom waved Mexican flags, Jim Gilchrist told the audience, "If this isn't a declaration of war, I don't know what is."[7] Members of white nationalist groups were also present and distributing literature in the auditorium.[8]

On May 12, 2005, the U.S. House of Representatives' Committee on Government Reform held a hearing to discuss border security. T.J. Bonner, national president of the National Border Patrol Council of the American Federation of Government Employees AFL-CIO, testified that the Minuteman Project was not the first group of citizens to "assemble to demand enforcement of our immigration laws," and that earlier such efforts had led to increased government attention, a dramatic increase in the number of Border Patrol agents, and a shift in undocumented patterns. Bonner noted that front-line Border Patrol employees "are very appreciative of the support shown by citizens who speak out for secure borders and additional resources to achieve that goal."[9]

Chris Simcox also testified at this hearing and opened with the following statement: "Almost four years after the terrible terrorist attacks upon our country on September 11, 2001, citizens of the United States remain concerned about our national security, specifically our outrageously porous international border with Mexico."[10]

He then went on to say how the "citizen effort has led to the capture, by the proper authorities" of undocumented migrants and cited statistics that are nowhere backed up. These conferences are just a few examples of what might be considered "legitimating activities" that have lent an air of acceptability to civilian border vigilante groups and have bestowed upon individuals such as Chris Simcox a mantle of expertise.[11]

To say that many speakers at these events are part of the anti-immigrant "movement" in the United States should not be understood as suggesting a simplistic portrayal of the large, diverse, and decentralized nature of what I refer to as the anti-immigrant movement. There is no overarching organization to which all of the individuals and groups who make up this movement belong. Rob Paral, a research fellow for the American Immigration Law Foundation in Washington, D.C., states that the "anti-forces" are largely unorganized—at least at the national level.[12] There are also chasms and divisions amongst some of the members of this movement.[13] However, there are also important linkages amongst individuals and organizations that constitute the "anti-forces." What I refer to as the anti-immigrant movement consists of those whom many would regard as extremists or fringe, as well as restrictionist organizations who profess to be research-oriented think tanks and are generally considered more respectable. Groups and members are connected to one another in various ways, primarily in their views on immigration and particularly in their advocacy for similar policies pertaining to undocumented immigration, guest worker programs, and border enforcement. Many of the groups reference one another in the "links" sections of their Web sites, though usually with a disclaimer about not necessarily endorsing the views of those organizations listed. They often attend and speak at the same conferences and publicize each other's events.

It is clear that the groups making up the anti-immigrant movement do not necessarily share identical ideologies and viewpoints on every single aspect of the immigration issue, nor do they operate as a unified political bloc. They include members of both major political parties, as well as those outside the mainstream parties.[14] Some groups focus on national security, others focus on population and the environment, while still others focus on national culture and identity.[15] However, in terms of their agendas and goals, a sufficient degree of commonality exists so as to justify using the term "movement." One frequently finds overlapping membership in one or more organizations and members of the various groups themselves use the term "social movement" to describe the network of organizations promoting an anti-immigrant agenda.[16] The border vigilante groups discussed in chapter 2, most notably Chris Simcox's Minuteman Civil Defense Corps and Jim Gilchrist's Minuteman Project, are part and parcel of this movement and have indeed lent strength to it as a whole. This is clearly illustrated in the comments of Rick Oltman and Tom Tancredo, noted above, that pertain to the significance of the April 2005 Minuteman Project to the overall movement. In turn, the anti-immigrant movement facilitates a degree of legitimation to border groups that otherwise might have been deemed insignificant, fringe, or extremist. The linkages with national security, especially after 9/11 are, in part, responsible for the increased strength of the anti-immigrant movement, though other factors are at work as well.

This chapter examines the more prominent groups and individuals that make up the anti-immigrant movement. I also explore three specific realms within which linkages have been made between this movement and other causes. These include: (1) the linking of immigration to national security by members of the anti-immigrant movement and the reciprocal taking-up of the immigration issue by members of the national security establishment, (2) the Christian connection that has surfaced recently as evidenced by the fact that several individuals and organizations that are part of the Christian right have recently taken up the anti-immigrant cause—though these connections were also present in earlier periods of history—and (3) connections with the white supremacist/nativist groups that support and actively promote an anti-immigrant agenda. My discussion of this last relationship does not necessarily mean that all of the groups or individuals discussed in this chapter or in chapter 2 have direct links with supremacist groups. I do, however, mean to suggest that the agenda anti-immigrant groups promote is inherently attractive to racist groups and, whether intentionally or not, attracts them to the cause.

## The Contemporary Anti-Immigrant Movement in the United States

One of the largest, oldest, and most well-known anti-immigrant organizations, which acts as something of an umbrella for the movement as a whole, is the Federation for American Immigration Reform (FAIR), a Washington, D.C.-based nonprofit organization. This is the closest thing to an overarching organization found in the anti-immigrant movement. It claims to have more than 198,000 members and supporters nationwide, with a satellite office in Los Angeles and field representatives across the country.[17] Its current chairwoman, Nancy Anthony, claims that FAIR is "front and center in what has emerged as one of the defining political issues of the early 21st century."[18] FAIR is the nation's first anti-immigrant policy institute and was formed in 1979 by John Tanton and other former members of Zero Population Growth, an environmental group. This marked the introduction of environmentalism into immigration debates and vice versa.[19] In 1982, Tanton—who has been referred to as the "founding father of America's modern anti-immigration movement"—also created U.S. Inc., whose purpose, according to the Southern Poverty Law Center, was to raise and channel funds to his anti-immigrant network.[20] The following year, he and California senator S.I. Hayakawa founded U.S. English.[21]

FAIR's stated goals are "to improve border security, to stop illegal immigration, and promote immigration levels consistent with the national interest—more traditional rates of about 300,000 a year."[22] While group members profess to advocate for fair immigration policies, their agenda is restrictionist and they have been linked to racist, anti-Latino, and even supremacist organizations.[23] Tanton, along with a few other FAIR board members, also founded a nationalist group called WITAN, short for "witenagemot" (an old English term meaning "council of wise men"). In 1988, several memos written by Tanton and then-executive director of FAIR Roger Conner were leaked. The memos were highly inflammatory, raising such questions as, "Will the present majority peaceably hand over its political power to a group that is simply more fertile?" and, "—perhaps this is the first instance in which those with their pants up are going to get caught by those with their pants down" and, "What are the differences in educability" between Hispanics and Asiatics?[24] In a January 2005 report, FAIR stated that "It is clear that there is a 'fifth column' movement in the United States that professes greater allegiance to a greater Mexico or a breakaway, separatist movement based on a Latino homeland. . . ."[25] FAIR's current executive director is Dan Stein, who puts out the Web-based Stein Report on immigration.

FAIR has received funding from the Pioneer Fund, which is infamous for its support of eugenics research in the pre–World War II era and its continued financial backing for racial segregation and racist science.[26] The Southern Poverty Law Center added FAIR to its list of hate groups in December 2007.[27]

After 9/11, FAIR led the way in forming a new coalition, United to Secure America, which launched a series of TV and print ads focusing on immigration. FAIR has given Glenn Spencer of American Patrol at least $11,000 in financial support.[28] FAIR is also behind the TV commercials aired as being run by the Coalition for the Future American Worker, which began in 2004.[29] These commercials focus on undocumented immigration and have been referred to as "borderline racist."[30] One of the ads centers around the Storm Lake meatpacking plant in Iowa and is based on a study published by the University of Kansas Press attesting to the drop in wages in the meatpacking industry.[31] While the facts relayed in the commercial are accurate, the message is strongly contested. The author of the study, Professor Michael Grey of the University of Iowa, attempted to have the commercial taken off the air—not because of factual inaccuracies, but because he disagreed "in the strongest terms possible with how they use this information to justify their borderline racist, anti-immigrant advertisements and political activities."[32] The president of the Iowa Federation of Labor, Mark Smith, said of the ad: "It's just racist stuff with no factual basis." Eventually, the ad was pulled by Iowa's *New York Times*-owned TV station, WHO-TV, after the station's general manager, Jim Boyer, called it "unnecessarily inflaming."[33] The spokesperson for the Coalition for the Future American Worker is Roy Beck, who is also head of NumbersUSA—another anti-immigrant group. Beck was a featured speaker at an annual conference of the white supremacist organization Council of Conservative Citizens, discussed below.[34]

FAIR was also a prominent player in the Proposition 200 campaign in Arizona. Proposition 200 was a ballot initiative that, among other things, required proof of citizenship to vote. It passed in November 2004 with 56 percent of the vote and became a catalyst for a rash of nationwide immigration measures aimed at denying undocumented migrants access to jobs, healthcare, homes, and legal protection. The state group Protect Arizona Now, which fought for passage of Proposition 200, was advised by a national advisory board chaired by Dr. Virginia Deane Abernathy, who held leadership positions in several organizations that advocate racial purity.[35] The passage of Proposition 200 and the 2005 Minuteman Project have been hailed by anti-immigrant leaders nationwide as the two events that most recently catapulted their movement to the forefront of the national agenda and made Arizona its epicenter.[36]

John Tanton is also the founder and publisher in charge of the Social Contract Press, a company he started in 1990 through which he published books, reports, and a journal—*The Social Contract*—out of his office for sixteen years.[37] Immigration issues are the main topic of discussion in the material published by this press. The links page of the Social Contract Press's Web site lists FAIR, the Center for Immigration Studies, American Renaissance, VDARE, and NumbersUSA, among other groups.[38] In 1996, Tanton coauthored a book with Wayne Lutton,

*The Immigration Invasion.* Lutton, editor of *The Social Contract,* is also an associate editor of *The Occidental Quarterly: A Journal of Western Thought and Opinion.* In its "Statement of Principles," *The Occidental Quarterly* states the following commitments: "The West is a cultural compound of our Classical, Christian, and Germanic past. The European identity of the United States and its people should be maintained. Immigration into the United States should be restricted to selected people of European ancestry."[39]

Lutton also serves as a trustee of the New Century Foundation, a think tank that publishes a monthly journal and maintains a Web site, both of which are called *American Renaissance.* The New Century Foundation was founded in 1990 by Jared Taylor and the journal is considered the leading intellectual journal of contemporary white nationalism.[40] The purpose of the journal, according to Taylor, "is to discuss issues that are of interest to whites."[41]

One of FAIR's more recent activities is the creation of Choose Black America (CBA). CBA was formed in May 2006 and is billed as a coalition of black leaders, businessmen, and academics. It is part of FAIR's efforts to dispel accusations of racism in the anti-immigrant movement. CBA's homepage states that "Mass illegal immigration has been the single greatest impediment to black advancement in this country over the past 25 years."[42] FAIR's July 2006 newsletter announced that it had "helped a coalition of black Americans make their voices heard in Washington, D.C."[43] However, several groups that monitor anti-immigrant groups, including Source Watch, the Southern Poverty Law Center, and the Center for New Democracy, report that FAIR's involvement is a bit more extensive and that CBA is actually a project of FAIR.[44] CBA's homepage lists the names of their media contacts as Ira Mehlman and Susan Wysoki. Mehlman is the media director for FAIR and Wysoki is a spokesperson for FAIR. CBA is well publicized by several of the anti-immigrant groups. A simple search on Google will yield stories lauding CBA on the Web sites of VDARE, American Renaissance, the Stein Report, and U.S. Border Control—to note just a few. The chairman of CBA is Dr. Frank Morris Sr., a longtime anti-immigrant activist. Morris sits on the board of the Center for Immigration Studies discussed below. Another member of the leadership of CBA is Ted Hayes, a Los Angeles homeless advocate, who has worked with Jim Gilchrist of the Minuteman Project.[45]

If FAIR is the umbrella of the anti-immigrant movement, the Center for Immigration Studies (CIS) can be considered its research arm and legitimating face. CIS presents itself as impartial and research oriented. It regularly publishes papers on immigration-related issues and its directors, Mark Krikorian and Steve Camarota, frequently testify on Capitol Hill and on various immigration forums. CIS reports, articles, studies, and books are widely cited by immigration researchers and frequently appear in the mainstream press. The group claims to give "first concern to the broad national interest" and to promote "a pro-immigrant, low immigration vision." CIS generally refrains from the more obviously nationalist, inflammatory rhetoric. However, the Southern Poverty Law Center, Political Research Associates, and the National Immigration Forum have labeled CIS an anti-immigrant group.[46] CIS has received funding from several influential foundations known for funding right-wing causes, including the Lynde and Harry Bradley Foundation, the Carthage Foundation, and the Sarah Scaife Foundation.[47] In response to the Immigrant Workers' Freedom Ride in 2003, Mark Krikorian told the *Miami Herald*, "Any event that advertises the participation of illegal aliens ought to be raided, and the illegal aliens deported."[48] CIS maintains an "employer sanctions database," which lists employers who have been cited for employing undocumented migrants.[49] In addition, CIS is not unconnected to FAIR—in fact, in 1985, FAIR helped found the Center for Immigration Studies.[50] Both Krikorian and Camarota praised the 2005 Minuteman Project, predicting that "more private citizens will volunteer to help monitor our neglected border with Mexico" and repeating the widespread but disputed assertion that the Minutemen stopped "almost all illegal crossings along a section of the border."[51] This latter claim has been rejected by the U.S. Border Patrol, which asserts that any reduction in illegal crossings can be attributed to Operation Stay Alert, which began on March 15, 2005 as a way of encouraging citizens to report illegal crossings to them.[52]

In 2005, the National Council of La Raza reported that CIS, along with FAIR, was organizing community groups in Dalton, Georgia that were hostile to Hispanics.[53] CIS shares the ideology of many anti-immigrant groups that "the high-immigration Right works hand-in-glove with the anti-American left."[54] Tom Barry suggests that CIS's rhetoric of environmental protection, access to jobs, and population control obscures its role in the campaign against immigrants and in favor of strict border controls and legislation.[55]

Another very prominent anti-immigrant organization is the American Immigration Control Foundation (AICF), also referred to as AIC, which was formed in 1983.[56] The AICF publishes and sells pamphlets, books, and monographs on various aspects of immigration. In 1987, the group published an edition of the infamous anti-immigration novel *The Camp of the Saints*, which was originally published in 1973 in France and eventually went out of print. In 1995, it was reissued by the anti-immigrant lobby with funding from Cordelia Scaife May, a Mellon heiress. The AICF and the Social Contract Press both republished and distributed it, and it was also pushed by FAIR.[57] This book tells the story of the third-world invasion of the West by a flotilla of ships loaded with poor people from India hoping to take advantage of the West's inability to control immigration. The theme in this piece of fiction is much the same as that of Pat Buchanan's latest non-fiction diatribe, *State of Emergency: The Third World Invasions and Conquest of America*. The AICF has also received funding from the Pioneer Fund—according to the Institute for the Study of Academic Racism, the AICF received more than $190,000 from the Pioneer Fund through 1998.[58] On May 12, 2006, the AICF organized a rally in Washington, D.C. to welcome Jim Gilchrist's Minuteman Project caravan that was traveling across the country gathering signatures for petitions protesting any form of amnesty being considered by the U.S. Senate.[59] The group advocated for even more restrictionist policies than were called for by House Bill 4437 of 2005, which sparked the nationwide pro-immigrant marches of the spring of 2006.[60] The AICF is opposed to the constitutionally guaranteed automatic citizenship for children born in the United States whose parents are undocumented, as is FAIR.[61]

The AICF is linked to the Council of Conservative Citizens (C of CC), which has its origins in the white citizens' councils of the 1960s and is considered the largest white supremacist organization in the United States.[62] Brent Nelson is a board member of the AICF and also sits as director of the C of CC, as well as serving on the editorial advisory board of its publication, *Citizen's Informer*.[63] While the AICF claims millions of members, including "citizens of all races, creeds, and colors," the Council of Conservative Citizens' statement of principles include the following statements:[64]

We believe that the United States derives from and is an integral part of European civilization and the European people and that the American people and government should remain European in their composition and character.

> We therefore oppose the massive immigration of non-European and non-Western peoples into the United States that threatens to transform our nation into a non-European majority in our lifetime.
> We also oppose all efforts to mix the races of mankind.[65]

The Southern Poverty Law Center reports that the AICF's leader, John Vinson, is an adviser to the C of CC.[66] Among the groups listed on the C of CC's links page is the infamously racist British Nationalist Party, the main right-wing party in Britain, which promotes an anti-immigrant agenda.[67] The Council of Conservative Citizens recently helped promote a visit to the United States by two Belgian politicians with the Vlaams Belang, a political party that Belgium's Supreme Court has declared racist.[68] The occasion was a forum sponsored by the Robert A. Taft Club, a right-wing organization. The forum was organized by Marcus Epstein, who is the executive director of both the American Cause Foundation, founded by Pat Buchanan, and the Team America political action committee, founded by Tom Tancredo. On the evening prior to the forum, the two Belgian politicians met with FAIR in Washington, D.C.[69]

According to the Southern Poverty Law Center, Rick Oltman, FAIR's Western regional coordinator, is also a member of the Council of Conservative Citizens.[70] Rick Oltman is widely known in anti-immigrant circles and speaks frequently at immigration conferences.[71] The Center for New Community reports that the Council of Conservative Citizen's winter 1997–98 edition of the newsletter *Citizen Informer* describes Oltman as a member. It goes on to say that in 1997, he shared the podium with the C of CC's Virginia Abernethy at a C of CC conference, and that at a January 17, 1998 anti-immigration rally in Cullman, Alabama, Oltman shared the podium with C of CC's leaders and William Burchfield, a onetime Alabama state leader of Thom Robb's Ku Klux Klan.[72] Oltman is also frequently present in the mainstream media. For example, he was part of a PBS *NewsHour* discussion on "Tightening the Borders" on January 1, 2002, along with Senator Dianne Feinstein, Richard Gephardt, and others.[73] Glenn Spencer's American Patrol, discussed in chapter 2, awarded Oltman the American Patrol's 2004 "Person of the Year" award, in part due to his work in helping to get Arizona's Proposition 200 on the ballot, saying, "The success of Proposition 200 is but one of many major contributions that Rick Oltman has made in the fight against illegal immigration."[74] In April 2006 at the Minutemen's second major border watch, Oltman presented Chris Simcox with a replica of the lantern used by Paul Revere during the Revolutionary War. In his field report, Stacy O'Connell—at the time Arizona state director of the Minuteman Civil Defense Corps—wrote, "Thanks Rick, you are a great patriot."[75] In 1996, the *Coastal Post* reported that Oltman was removed from his post as chairperson of the Republican Central Committee in Marin County, California for "publicly agreeing with the beating of illegals in Southern California," though he was later reinstated.[76]

One of the major supporters of the Minuteman Project is the Congressional Immigration Reform Caucus (CIRC), formed by U.S. House of Representative members in 1999 and led by Tom Tancredo. In April 2005, the CIRC sent an observation team to the Minuteman Project in April 2005 that later submitted a glowing report.[77] On April 27 of the same year, the CIRC hosted a "media availability" event with organizers and participants of the Minuteman Project in the Rayburn Gold Room, the purpose of which was to "discuss successes and direction of the Minutemen."[78] At this meeting, Congressman Phil Gingrey of Georgia said, "I encourage other citizens to support this cause and defend our nation." J.D Hayworth of Arizona said, "Now it is up to every American to get involved in this critical struggle to preserve our security and our sovereignty by demanding that this administration and this Congress stop thinking about amnesty and start enforcing our immigration laws."[79]

Tancredo has long been an advocate of restrictionist immigration policies and has been accused of having ties to white supremacist organizations.[80] The Council of Conservative Citizens lists Tancredo on its links page and although it states that "links do not necessarily constitute an endorsement of any content," most of the sites listed are white nationalist and anti-immigrant groups such as Protect Arizona Now, Save Our State, the British National Party, Vlaams Belang of Belgium, and the Social Contract Press. Tancredo's writings have been published on the Web site of the white supremacist National Vanguard.[81] In September 2006, neoconfederate group League of the South hosted a barbeque in honor of Tancredo.[82] Proceeds from the fifteen-dollar-a-plate fundraiser went to Americans Have Had Enough, a South Carolina–based nonprofit headed by Tancredo.[83] Tancredo attracted additional attention when he referred to Miami as a "Third World country," suggesting that it was an example of how "the nature of America can be changed by uncontrolled immigration."[84] It is tempting to dismiss these examples as extremist fringe and, while disturbing, ultimately not very consequential.

Tancredo has long been considered so radical in his views on immigration that President Bush Sr.'s advisor Karl Rove told him not "to darken the doorstep of the White House."[85] However, Tancredo and his views have undergone a significant degree of "legitimation" over the past several years. He has received an enormous amount of media exposure, spoken more than a thousand times on talk shows, and frequently appeared on television news programs.[86] He has exercised a considerable amount of influence over immigration policy and was crucial in producing the border security bill passed by the House in 2005, H.B. 4437—also known as the Sensenbrenner Bill. Norman Orenstein, a political analyst with the American Enterprise Institute, says of Tancredo's role in the contemporary immigration debate: "It wouldn't have been dealt with this level of intensity or even urgency if it weren't for him."[87] Tancredo's anti-immigrant book *In Mortal Danger: The Battle for America's Border and Security* was published by WorldNetDaily in 2006.

David Horowitz's right-wing Center for the Study of Popular Culture has also recently picked up on the immigration issue, co-sponsoring a daylong conference in August 2005 along with FAIR and the Coalition for Immigration Reform in California. Speakers at this conference included Tom Tancredo, Jim Gilchrist, Mark Krikorian of the Center for Immigration Studies, George Borjas—a professor of economics and social policy at Kennedy School of Government at Harvard—and prominent neoconservative Frank Gaffney Jr., among others.[88] The point to be noted here is that there was a close connection between prominent members of border vigilante groups such as Simcox and Gilchrist and the broader anti-immigrant movement, as well as between these individuals, the movement, and some policy makers and academics. This is not to say that all of the policy makers and academics share the views of Gilchrist, Simcox, and Tancredo. It is important, however, to note that these individuals have gained what is arguably considered by many to be a "legitimate" as well as "expert" voice in the immigration debate, and they have been given numerous forums through which to espouse their positions on immigration.

The above discussion alludes to some significant connections that have been made in recent years between immigration and other sociopolitical issues. Three issue areas stand out: national security, the Christian right, and white supremacy/nativism. Various connections are evident between individuals or groups in the anti-immigrant movement (including those who are a part of border vigilante groups) and individuals or groups connected to these three issue areas. These connections are significant for several reasons. Common themes can be found and often these work in a reciprocal fashion to the mutual advantage of both the anti-immigrant movement and the groups focused on these other issues, which can importantly work to lend legitimacy to the anti-immigrant cause. This is most evident in the case of national security. In other cases, the anti-immigrant cause can be used to recruit members and garner support for other issues because of shared concerns. This seems to be increasingly the case when it comes to white supremacist groups.

## Connection I: National Security

Here's what I worry about: the al-Qaida.[89]

At various times throughout history, the issues of immigration and national security have been linked to one another and security concerns have been used to promote restrictionist positions.[90] This connection existed long before the September 11, 2001, attacks on the United States. Anti-immigrant politics were fueled in the 1990s when the 1993 bombing of the World Trade Center and the assassination of two CIA employees in Virginia by undocumented migrants from Pakistan helped catapult the immigration issue to unprecedented national importance.[91] In 1999, FAIR engaged in a campaign against Michigan senator Spencer Abraham because of his pro-immigrant stance. FAIR ran an ad in the *Grand Rapids Press* with the headline "Why is a U.S. Senator Trying to Make it Easy for Osama bin Laden to Export Terrorism to the U.S.?" The ad contained a picture of Senator Abraham alongside a photo of Osama bin Laden.[92] The events of September 11, 2001, and the subsequent overwhelming emphasis on national security, while not solely responsible for the resurgence of anti-immigrant sentiment, did breathe new life into the movement and arguably made the U.S. public more receptive to some of the restrictionist ideas. Media coverage of anti-immigrant grassroots organizing increased, as did congressional bills and the constituency base of those advocating strict immigration enforcement.[93] U.S. Representative Duncan Hunter of California expressed the following sentiments: "Prior to September 11, 2001, illegal immigration was considered a regional issue without national implications. We quickly learned on that day, however, that this is a national issue, affecting each and every American, not just those living in border communities like San Diego County."[94]

Hunter's view resonated widely, and anti-immigrant forces were able to link their agenda to national security by drawing on the fears and uncertainty that resulted from the attacks.[95] Membership in Tancredo's Immigration Reform Caucus increased significantly from sixteen members when it was first formed to the current eighty-nine members.[96] At the Scottsdale conference noted in the opening to this chapter, Arizona Representative J.D. Hayworth proclaimed passionately in reference to stopping undocumented immigration, "This may be the last thing we do as a free people."[97] The attacks on the United States functioned to cement the connection between immigration and national security/terrorism regardless of how dubious and unsupported it was by empirical evidence.

Articulations of this connection increased in several arenas. Shortly after 9/11, Tom Tancredo introduced a bill that would have imposed a moratorium on new immigration, asking, "How many people in this country have to lose their lives before we come to the understanding that defense of the nation begins at the defense of our borders?"[98] Tancredo's Immigration Reform Caucus' Web site features two documentaries entitled *Terrorist Alley* and *The Terrorist Next Door*, in which Tancredo warns, without evidence, that the Mexican border is an open door to Islamic terrorists.[99] Richard Lamm, policy advisor to the Foundation for the Defense of Democracies and a member of the board of advisors of FAIR, suggested after 9/11 that "we must confront the relationship between immigration and terrorism."[100] It is reasonable to suggest that this translated into support—or at least sympathy for—the cause of border vigilante groups. A statewide poll conducted in Arizona by Arizona State University's Walter Cronkite School of Journalism and Mass Communication in April 2005—during the Minutemen's first operation—found that 57 percent of those interviewed supported the Minutemen Project.[101]

National security continues to be a major focus of border vigilante groups and the anti-immigrant movement. In response to the nationwide immigrant rights marches on April 10, 2006, the Minuteman Civil Defense Corps Web site posted notice of a counter protest in Washington, D.C., sponsored by 9/11 Families for a Secure America which read, "9/11 Families for a Secure America Invites victims of terrorism and other crimes committed by illegal aliens to a protest in Washington D.C." The body of the invitation groups together "the 9/11 attacks, other terrorist attacks, street violence, and motor vehicle crimes" with undocumented immigration.[102]

The linking of immigration and national security is not without consequence. For example, Transactional Records Access Clearinghouse (TRAC), a research group connected to Syracuse University, reports that federal prosecutions for immigration violations more than doubled in 2004 as compared with 2001 and that immigration matters now represent the single-largest group of all federal prosecutions, about one-third of the total. Interestingly, the Department of Homeland Security, which was created in the wake of 9/11 with a core mission of fighting terrorism, is very much involved in the prosecution of traditional immigration cases that appear to have very little to do with terrorism. TRAC reports that only seven out of 37,765 prosecutions arising out of its immigration enforcement were classified as involving international terrorism in fiscal year 2004 and only one out of 20,771 in fiscal year 2003.[103] The connection between immigration and national security is a hallmark theme among the numerous anti-immigrant groups, as illustrated in Mark Krikorian's 2004 article published in *The National Interest*, "Keeping Terror Out: Immigration and Asymmetric Warfare."[104]

The connection made between national security and immigration is also illustrated by overlapping membership and support for organizations on both fronts. The Center for Security Policy, mentioned at the beginning of this chapter, is a case in point. The Center's national security advisory council "serves as a key instrument for the networking, information sharing, paper production, and recommendation dissemination that has been the Center for Security Policy raison d'etre."[105] According to the Center's Web site, "The principal audience for such materials is the U.S. security policy-making community (the executive and legislative branches, the armed forces, and appropriate independent agencies), corresponding organizations in key foreign governments, the press (domestic and international), the global business and financial community and interested individuals in the public at large."[106] The Center was instrumental in starting the group Family Security Matters, and Frank Gaffney is on its board of advisors.[107] The Center has also received several grants to support the Family Security Matters Network.[108] Family Security Matters publishes articles on its Web site that focus on terrorism, security, and immigration and that link these three issues to one another. Michael Cutler, who is an advisor to Family Security Matters and also a fellow at the Center for Immigration Studies, writes that more Americans are killed by "illegal aliens" than by the Iraq war.[109]

Alan Keyes, a member of the Center for Security Policy's national security advisory council, is also closely connected to Chris Simcox's Minuteman Civil Defense Corps. He has long been a supporter of the MCDC and has spoken at several of their events.[110] The Minuteman Civil Defense Corps political action committee is a project of the Declaration Alliance, a tax-exempt charity founded by Alan Keyes, and the homepage of the political action committee displays the Declaration Alliance logo.[111] Keyes also started the Declaration Foundation, which describes itself as "a non-profit educational organization, dedicated to restoring the principles of the Declaration of Independence to their rightful place in American life. It is not a political organization, and takes no position on candidates or elections." The group lists one of its goals as "to maintain our website as a civics and education resource center for Declarationists."[112] Its homepage features an advertisement for Simcox's Minuteman Border Project and a call for Minuteman volunteers for the MCDC with the well-known Uncle Sam logo pointing a finger at the reader and captioned with the words, "I Want You." The Declaration Alliance defines itself as a "civic public policy and issues advocacy organization that aggressively defends the Founding principles of the American Republic." Its goals include overturning *Roe v. Wade*, the right to "publicly acknowledge the authority of the Creator God," and "protect, defend and uphold our national security and sovereignty, at home and abroad . . . and . . . secure America's borders against foreign invasion."[113] The group's homepage also features the advertisement for the Minuteman Border Project and refers to Sept. 11, 2001, under the heading of "Why We Fight and Why We Will Win." Keyes' Declaration Alliance political action committee is the "official campaign and ballot initiative arm of the tax-exempt Declaration Alliance."

The ways in which national security and immigration have been linked, especially since September 11, 2001, illustrate that there is often a rather blurry line between *national security* and *societal security*, and that they can work in a symbiotic fashion. Both depend upon the notion of an enemy.

### Connection II: The Christian Right

The link between Keyes' organizations and the Minuteman Civil Defense Corps calls attention to another issue area that has recently become connected to the anti-immigrant movement, that is, the Christian right. Many Christian groups are strong supporters of migrant rights, and even within the more conservative religious groups, there is not a unified

position on immigration.[114] However, an important segment of the religious right has recently aligned itself with the anti-immigrant movement and with specific groups and individuals in that movement. In April 2006, the Family Research Council (FRC), a leading Christian and conservative group, hosted an immigration conference titled "Faith, Culture, and Law in the Immigration Debate" in Washington, D.C.[115] Amongst the featured panelists were Tom Tancredo and Mark Krikorian.[116]

The Secure Borders Coalition is an alliance of Christian right groups and other conservative organizations such as Accuracy in Media and the Swiftboat Veterans for Truth, as well as the Minuteman Civil Defense Corps. Both Chris Simcox and Alan Keyes are members of the Coalition. In June 2006, the Coalition issued a pledge to withhold support for lawmakers who voted in favor of "amnesty" for undocumented migrants and who supported S2611, the Senate's 2006 "compromise" immigration bill that was quite a bit less restrictive than the House Bill noted earlier, H.B. 4437—though it was still unsatisfactory for many immigrant rights groups. Forty-three conservative leaders within the Coalition signed the pledge, including Bay Buchanan of Tom Tancredo's Team America and sister of Pat Buchanan, David Horowitz, Alan Keyes, Mark Krikorian of the Center for Immigration Studies, and Chris Simcox. The pledge accused political leaders who supported S2611 of selling out "our sovereignty" and surrendering "our national identity for ethnic votes." It called for a "policy of attrition of the illegal immigration population through strong enforcement of our immigration laws."[117] Another signer was Phyllis Schlafly of the Eagle Forum, one of the oldest religious right groups, founded in 1972. Schlafly, well known for her anti-gay, anti-abortion stances, has joined the anti-immigrant chorus. In July 2006, she testified in a hearing before the Subcommittee on Immigration, Border Security, and Claims on the Committee on the Judiciary House of Representatives in opposition to S1. Schlafly has recently been connected to Jim Gilchrist (who is not a member of the Secure Borders Coalition). He was a featured guest at the thirty-fifth annual Eagle Forum Conference in September, 2006.[118] Schlafly's syndicated commentaries are also posted on Tom Tancredo's Team America homepage.[119]

In January 2007, several leading Christian conservative groups formed another coalition on immigration, Families First on Immigration.[120] According to Media Transparency, Manuel Miranda is responsible for putting together this coalition.[121] The coalition's membership is reportedly bigger and broader than that of the Secure Borders Coalition, with

members including: Paul Weyrich, president and founder of the Free Congress Research and Education Foundation, Donald Wildmon of the American Family Association, Gary Bauer of the American Conservative Union, and David Keene and Lou Sheldon of the Traditional Values Coalition.[122] Among other things, the group has taken up the cause of eradicating the birthright citizenship guaranteed under the Fourteenth Amendment: in early January 2007, members sent letters to President Bush and leaders of the new Democrat-controlled Congress urging them "to adopt a grand compromise on the divisive issues that includes strong border security, an amnesty for illegals already here who are relatives of citizens and an end to birthright citizenship."[123]

Anti-immigrant religious groups often focus on family, cultural values, and the identity of the nation. They link these with a particular form of Christianity. This is evident in the goals of The Declaration Alliance noted above. Thomas Fleming of the Christian-oriented Rockford Institute says that "the cultural ambience aspect of the immigration debate is the only one that interests me."[124] In the Rockford Institute's magazine, he wrote, "Whatever we may say in public, most of us do not much like Mexicans, whom we regard as too irrational, too violent, too passionate."[125] The issue of culture, the family, and national identity is also a prominent theme amongst other anti-immigrant groups and individuals. This is perhaps most obviously exemplified by claims that undocumented migrants are a danger to the children of the United States. Underlying this claim is a fear that migrants pose a threat to the very identity and integrity of this country. A statement by Mothers Against Illegal Aliens, discussed in chapter 2, supports this: "We must not allow strangers to determine the future course of this Nation and as such the future course of our Legal Children."[126] Anti-immigration white supremacist groups also play upon notions of family and "Christian" values, linking these with race. American Renaissance features a picture of a toddler under the heading "By the Time she's 40 she'll be a racial minority."[127] The Ku Klux Klan is another group that touts family and religious values. Big bold letters on its Web site state: "Welcome to the Ku Klux Klan. Bringing a Message of Hope and Deliverance to White Christian America!" On May 12, 2007, the "message of the day"—which may be read daily upon entering the site—pertained to the "immigration crisis," stating: "We are now in the midst of a steady decline in America. It coincides with the decline of the white population."[128]

## Connection III: White Supremacy/Nativism

> "Alan, there are supremacist groups out there of all races, colors,
> and creeds. It's not just white supremacists. Why are you picking
> on them? There are brown. There are purple. There are red."[129]

Arguably one of the most disturbing connections to surface is the relationship between the anti-immigrant movement and white supremacist/nativist individuals and organizations.

Groups such as Simcox's Minuteman Civil Defense Corps, Gilchrist's Minuteman Project, and Glenn Spencer's American Patrol say they are careful to warn racists that they are not welcome. A recent Minuteman Project rally in Rancho Cucamonga, California, was called off when members of the Ku Klux Klan showed up to support the organization.[130] Efforts like this on the part of border vigilante groups to shake images of them as racist may be sincere. However, there is evidence that the widespread anti-immigrant sentiment has provided fertile ground for individuals and groups that promote racist, white supremacist ideologies.[131] Some of the connections have already been alluded to above. The ideology and motivations of the border vigilante groups are attractive to groups and individuals who espouse racist ideas. Many of the slogans on Web sites and signs displayed at anti-immigrant rallies are identical to those of white supremacist groups. For example, the Web site www.put troopsontheborder.com, which is sponsored by the Ku Klux Klan, displays calls for putting the military on the border and warnings of "alien invasion." This message is indistinguishable from those on the Web sites of anti-immigrant—but ostensibly not white supremacist—groups.

Supremacist individuals and groups have made their presence felt in the overall movement. Even prior to the well-publicized 2005 Minuteman Project, white supremacists were applauding civilian border patrol groups. On December 1, 2002, Stormfront—the leading white supremacist blog—posted the following: "WOW!!! Newspaper owner Chris Simcox openly forming a militia to patrol the U.S. border and stop the Mexican invasion." The posting goes on to say that "he is openly calling all White men to the front lines to do battle! His group seeks nothing less than an end to the Browning of America."[132] In November 2004, Stormfront posted information about the upcoming April 2005 border watch. This posting notes that "this will not be a White racialist project, per se, and all that are concerned with our wide open borders are encouraged to apply."[133] The FBI expressed concern about these groups in March 2005, the month before the April Minuteman Project border operation. Minuteman organizers claimed that they turned over three people to the FBI, though this has not been confirmed. The April 2005 Minuteman Project was posted on the Aryan Nation's Web site's calendar of white power events.[134] White Revolution member Ben Vinyard posted a "Minuteman Update" on White Revolution's Web site, "bringing behind the scenes updates from the White activists' 'battlefield,' " and referring to the Minuteman operation as "The White patriots along the Naco Border."[135] White Revolution is a white supremacist group that seeks to "secure the existence of our people and a future for White children by creating the opportunity for the establishment of a government which has only the interests of our people in mind when deciding on its foreign and domestic policies."[136] In June 2006, the Ku Klux Klan held an anti-immigrant rally in Midland, Texas. Steven Edwards, leader of the Empire Knights of the Ku Klux Klan of Texas, said: "This country was made by white Europeans for white Europeans." Echoing various border vigilante groups, he also said that "a wall or a fence should be put up around the country."[137] In June 2006, two white pride groups organized anti-immigrant rallies in Nashua and Hudson, New Hampshire. On June 11, members of North East White Pride demonstrated in front of Nashua City Hall. On July 2, members of North East White Pride and White Revolution gathered in Library Park in Hudson.[138] In July 2006, the San Angelo chapter of the Ku Klux Klan planned a rally against undocumented migration in Amarillo.[139]

These are just a few of the numerous examples of white supremacists taking up the anti-immigrant cause. There are additional connections that may not generate headlines, but that arguably run deeper than the above and are equally disturbing. These other connections are with members of what Carol Swain refers to as the "new white nationalism" in America. She suggests that this movement, "while sharing much in common with the older style of white racist and white supremacy movement, and drawing upon important white supremacist beliefs . . . is potentially broader in its appeal."[140] The new white nationalists seek to protect "their God-given right to their distinct cultural, political, and genetic identity as white Europeans," an identity they believe is threatened by, among other things, large-scale immigration into the United States from non-white nations.[141] The individuals who are part of this phenomenon are generally better educated than old-style racists and often are able to pass themselves off as mainstream conservatives.[142] One of the more prominent members of the new white nationalism is Jared Taylor, editor of *American Renaissance.* Mark Potok of the Southern Poverty Law Center refers to Taylor as "the cultivated, cosmopolitan face of white supremacy."[143] American Renaissance's Web site features links to Glenn Spencer's American Patrol and the American Immigration Control Foundation and posts stories and announcements of various border campaigns. In a 2003 symposium on white nationalism, Taylor argued that "a preference for people of one's own group is natural, normal, and healthy," and that this is one of the reasons why a thorough overhaul of immigration is necessary. ". . . [I]f race is a legitimate criterion, why should whites (or blacks) welcome the arrival of Asians and Hispanics, who are alien to both?"[144] Taylor has suggested that the work of anti-immigration interest groups "tends to assist the survival of the white man."[145]

Jared Taylor is also one of the current directors of the National Policy Institute, whose former media director, Peter Gemma, was paid $7,740 by the U.S. Immigration Reform Political Action Committee in October 2004 for "clerical and administrative work."[146] The USIRP was established by FAIR in 1993 in order to identify and support candidates for public office who support FAIR's position on immigration. On its homepage, the National Policy Institute poses the question, regarding white Americans: "Isn't it about time someone spoke for us?" Gemma also served as a senior staff member for Pat Buchanan's 2000 presidential campaign, and in February 2004 spoke at a meeting in Virginia of the Institute for Historical Review, the leading holocaust-denial organization in the United States.[147] The current president of the board of directors of USIRP is Mary Lou Tanton, FAIR founder John Tanton's wife.

The relationship between the anti-immigrant movement and white supremacist and hate groups has recently received attention from various rights groups. In October 2006, anti-immigrant activist and Arizona Representative Russell Pearce sent an e-mail to supporters in which he copied an article from white separatist group the National Alliance's Web site. The article was titled, "Who Rules America? The Alien Grip on Our News and Entertainment Media Must Be Broken."[148] In February 2007, the Anti-Defamation League published a report on *The Ku Klux Klan Today,* reporting that the debate on immigration has become the Klan's major recruiting tool.[149] Many Ku Klux Klan groups have attempted to take advantage of the anxieties about immigration that seem to be in the

minds of many Americans, "using anti-immigrant sentiments for recruitment and propaganda purposes and to attract publicity."[150] The
Anti-Defamation League (ADL) reports that Ku Klux Klan groups expe-
rienced a resurgence in 2006 in areas where they have traditionally been
strong, as well as expansion in areas where they did not previously have a
strong presence.[151] At a seminar hosted by the ADL in Phoenix, Detective
Matt Browning of the Mesa, Arizona, Police Department said he had
spent the last twelve years working undercover with three border militia
groups and six white supremacist organizations, reporting that every
meeting revolved around immigration.[152] Lisa Navarrete of the National
Council of La Raza said that "the atmosphere has never been as poi-
sonous as it has been in the last few years."[153]

There is, of course, no way to be certain of the sincerity behind efforts
by groups such as the MCDC and the Minuteman Project to keep racists
out. "They cannot honestly say that they are doing this not knowing who
these people are," says Detective Browning, referring to the presence of
racists within border vigilante organizations.[154] The nature of their cause
is inherently attractive to white supremacists. A case in point is that of
J.T. Ready, former Mesa City Council candidate and member of the
original 2005 Minuteman Project. Ready spoke at a rally for the opening
of the project, saying, "Our very republic is teetering on the edge."[155]
Ready is also a registered member of New Saxon, "an online community
for whites by whites."[156] His page features numerous photos of him,
including one in which he is looking through binoculars on patrol at the
April 2005 border operation, and another at an Americans First rally,
which he organized at the Mexican Consulate in Phoenix on April 22,
2006.[157] His New Saxon maxim is: "We must create white families or
perish." "Race mixing" is one of his turn-offs.[158] Ready was amongst
the advertised participants attending the rally at Arizona Senator John
Kyle's Phoenix office on May 21, 2007, to protest the latest Senate immigration bill.[159]

The ideas that sustain the anti-immigrant movement today do not
operate in a vacuum. The history of opposition to migrants is rife with
connections to nativist and white supremacist sentiments.[160] Writer Max
Blumenthal tells of a conversation in 2005 with former Ku Klux Klan
leader David Duke. Referring to the 1970s, when he was attempting to
refine the image of the Klan, Duke said, "You know, people called me
crazy then for what I said about immigration, but I sound like every
Republican today, and a lot of Democrats, and no one gives me any

credit for that. And not only that, I conducted the first civilian border patrol."[161] This is not to say that every individual who is opposed to immigration shares the ideologies of white supremacists. It is, however, to suggest that powerful ideas about culture, national identity, and race have historically been intertwined, and that this enables opposition to immigration to operate across a broad (and often disturbing) spectrum, from which it garners strength. Racist connections are clearly present in the contemporary anti-immigrant movement.

# 4

# Spreading the Message

Publicity has been key to the organization and success of the anti-immigrant movement. Organizers of the 2005 Minuteman Project showed themselves to be incredibly savvy in terms of publicizing and garnering support for their border watches as well as for disseminating the general themes that characterize their organizations. However, this shrewdness must also be understood within a context in which various media outlets were already fairly quick to pick up on border stories. The effort of the project's organizers was aided by the fact that immigration had already attracted a great deal of media attention. The situation on the Arizona-Mexico border especially had been receiving a great deal of attention as it became the major crossing point for undocumented migrants. Prior to 9/11, much of the media coverage had focused on talks between President Bush and President Vicente Fox of Mexico regarding a guest worker program. Almost immediately after the 9/11 attacks, immigration-related coverage began to focus on national security-related issues. Chris Simcox's October famous 2002 "call to arms," published in the *Tombstone Tumbleweed,* was picked up on by news outlets across the country.[1] The following day, the *National Review* published an editorial praising Simcox and quoting the Second Amendment of the U.S. Constitution: "A well-regulated Militia being necessary to the security of a free state, the right of the People to keep and bear arms shall not be abridged."[2] Stories of Simcox's Civil Homeland Defense (as it was then called) were reported in numerous newspapers, including the *Arizona Daily Star*, the *San Francisco Chronicle*, the *Nation*, and Reuters.[3] In 2003, the *Los Angeles Times* ran a "Special to the Times" story on Chris Simcox and the "border militia" in Arizona.[4] In addition to coverage of Simcox's group, other civilian border groups had been reported on previously, especially in the local presses.[5] So, in an important sense, the Minuteman Project stepped into a realm that was already attracting significant media attention.

Nonetheless, the April 2005 Minuteman Project was an extraordinary media event and arguably the project *as* media event exceeded its significance as an act of border enforcement. Some have suggested that there was as much of a media presence in southeastern Arizona as there were volunteers for the project itself. Prior to its commencement on April 1, numerous newspapers ran stories of the coming event and various Internet sites posted information on the watch. On November 1, 2004, a recruitment announcement was sent out by Jim Gilchrist on Frosty Wooldridge's Web site asking volunteers to join him in Tombstone in the spring of 2005 to "protect our country from a 40-year-long invasion across our southern border with Mexico."[6] The media almost immediately started reporting on the planned border operation. In addition to local newspapers, the national press reported on the planned event. As early as January 2005, Reuters reported that the organizers of the Minuteman Project were recruiting volunteers and in February 2005, the *Washington Post* reported that "nearly 500 volunteers have already joined the Minuteman Project."[7] Numerous other national newspapers publicized the planned event, including the *Washington Times* and *The Christian Science Monitor.* A few days before the project commenced, BBC News ran a story.[8]

The event itself was covered by all the major news outlets, including the *Los Angeles Times,* the *San Antonio Express,* and FOX News. Extensive coverage continued throughout the month of April 2005 and continued subsequently as the number and activities of border vigilante groups grew and as undocumented immigration continued to be one of the major contemporary issues. In May 2005, Salon.com featured a lengthy story (of eleven printed pages) on Chris Simcox.[9] Even the *New Yorker,* which is aimed at a relatively sophisticated readership, has published articles on civilian border vigilantes, reporting in December 2005 on Chris Simcox's visit to Babylon, Long Island for a recruiting drive.[10] News coverage continues to be extensive.

This chapter examines the various outlets that have been used to "spread the word(s)" of border vigilantes and the anti-immigrant movement. These include conservative TV news, cable news, talk radio, the Internet, television, and books. These mediums have been instrumental in the perpetuation of certain themes that characterize the ways in which the issue of undocumented migration is understood and spoken about. It is in this sense that these outlets play an important part in the web of exclusionary rhetoric that underlies contemporary vigilantism. Clearly, immigration is currently an extremely divisive topic and vehement disagreement exists between pro- and anti-immigrant groups, as well as amongst members positioned on each of these sides. While alternative perspectives are presented in some media outlets, the messages disseminated by anti-immigrant groups have resonated widely with the mainstream press and general public. Whether directly or indirectly, intentionally or unintentionally, the more mainstream media often replicates the themes of border groups such as the Minuteman Project and the Minuteman Civil Defense Corps. One result has been a certain framing of the immigration issue that amplifies the sense of crisis associated with it and portrays undocumented migrants as the perpetuators of this crisis and by virtue of this, at least the potential enemy. This is not to say that the message has been uniformly received and uncritically accepted. Rather, the purpose of this chapter is to suggest that the "Minuteman perspective" has received widespread coverage that has enabled the group's message(s) to spread and to a significant degree to be accepted by sufficient numbers of people so as to preclude immigration "reform" that does not contain a strong element of "punishment" for those living in the United States without the proper documents. Coverage has also made more popular a major emphasis on border enforcement.

In a concise but classic book, Murray Edelman examines the construction and uses of the *political spectacle*. Drawing upon the ideas of Michele Foucault and other critical theorists, Edelman suggests that political problems often come into discourse and therefore into existence not because they are simply *there*, but rather because they are reinforcements of ideology. The ways in which political problems are defined and talked about constructs a social reality and the human beings who inhabit that social reality. This is certainly the case with undocumented migration. Of course, this should not be taken to suggest that there are no "real" and significant issues that need to be addressed. Rather, it is to suggest that what those issues *are* is not self-evident. Issues and problems often come to be regarded as self-evident through a process in which certain messages, themes, and "realities" are disseminated. In addition to the spreading of these things through the various outlets within the border vigilante and anti-immigrant movements, the writing about and reporting of this issue contributes to a political spectacle, within which undocumented migrants (and sometimes all migrants) are portrayed as "alien," dangerous, and thus at least potential enemies.[11] This chapter is not meant to be an exhaustive examination of all media outlets and all the coverage of civilian border and anti-immigrant groups. Instead, it is intended to provide a glimpse into the ways in which various media outlets have functioned to spread the messages of these groups and have facilitated the rather loud voice they have had in recent years.

## Television

During the first two weeks of the 2005 Minuteman Project, Jim Gilchrist and Chris Simcox appeared on Fox TV's *Hannity and Colmes* a total of seven times. Other supporters of the project, such as Tom Tancredo and J.D. Hayworth, also appeared. During the same time period, only one opposing view was presented, that of Mike Nicely, chief of the U.S. Border Patrol in Tucson, who reported that members of the Minuteman Project were tripping border sensors and thus having a negative impact on Border Patrol operations.[12] On the April 18 *Hannity and Colmes* show, Gilchrist claimed a 94-percent reduction in apprehensions. On the same show, Simcox suggested that the Minuteman Project had created "a model that works."[13] Hannity praised them, saying that they had "set up a rigid standard" and were "humanitarians first," feeding "people that are hungry" and offering "water to people that are thirsty." Co-host Alan Colmes described the Minuteman Project as "hugely successful."[14] Chris Simcox appeared on this show again on April 26, 2005, along with UCLA Professor Raúl Hinojosa. Prior to introducing Simcox, the show ran a video of the U.S.-Mexico border filmed near Naco, Arizona, by Simcox over the course of the previous year. Colmes said: "And joining us now from Capitol Hill to tell us about this powerful video, Minuteman organizer Chris Simcox. Chris, welcome back to the show."[15]

After discussing various segments of the video, which showed crossing paths and migrants coming over the border, the hosts and guests took a newsbreak and returned. Hannity said: ". . . and also joining us is UCLA professor, president of No Borders, Inc., Raúl Hinojosa." However, before turning to or greeting Professor Hinojosa, he continued his discussion with Simcox:

"First, Chris, I did want to point out on this video in particular here, this was all shot at night. And by the Border Patrol's own estimates, they acknowledge that four or five million people that they're not getting are coming into the United States each year, correct?"

"That's correct," Simcox replied. "And we can document that; we can account for that. You see by the video how many people that we've documented that have slipped through the Border Patrol's fingers."

With no welcome or greeting, Hannity turns to Hinojosa:

"Mr. Hinojosa, do you not see, do you not understand that if people are coming over—let's say they have just the motive that they want a job and a better life—do you not see if we don't control our borders, that the enemies of this country could cross over with dangerous weapons and perhaps wreak havoc on our cities? Do you not understand that?"

Hinojosa attempts a response: "I think what this video is really showing you is . . ."

Hannity: "I didn't ask you about that. I asked you—answer my question."

Hinojosa attempted to continue with his response: ". . . that this country is losing its capacity to have a rational debate on its problems . . ."

Hannity: "Mr. Hinojosa, I don't have a lot of time."

Hinojosa continued, with Hannity again interrupting: "I won't ask you another question if you don't respond to my question . . ."

To point out the somewhat obvious, what we see in this conversation is not only a noticeable difference in terms of the overall respect accorded to Simcox versus that shown toward Hinojosa, but a bestowal of expertise and legitimacy on Simcox and the Minuteman and a cross-examination-style approach to questioning Hinojosa. Hinojosa's credentials, which include degrees in economics, anthropology, and political science—as well as the authorship of numerous articles on international trade, investment, and migration relations between the United States and Latin America and the Pacific Rim—were discounted. He was not even given an opportunity to present a position. Simcox became the instant and reliable expert. He was accorded the legitimacy to speak on the accuracy of U.S. Border Patrol statistics. In contrast, Raúl Hinojosa was treated as suspect, as someone who either did not understand the seriousness of the situation or who refused to respond to Hannity's question.

A year later, Simcox used the *Hannity and Colmes* show to deliver his ultimatum to President Bush. He appeared on the show on phone from Nogales, Arizona, on April 19, 2006, saying: ". . . we're going to give the president an ultimatum to—to declare a state of emergency and deploy the National Guard and military reserves or by the 25th of May or Memorial Day weekend, we're going to break ground and we're going to start helping landowners to build a double layer security fence along their properties, because the federal government refuses to protect them."[16]

On April 9, 2006, the day before the nationwide pro-immigrant marches, Phoenix's Fox 10 *Newsmaker Sunday* morning show featured

Chris Simcox along with Elias Bermudez of the migrant rights group Sin Fronteras. Fox's local anchor, John Hook, interviewed Simcox and Bermudez. At one point, Hook turned to Bermudez and asked, "You came here illegally how many years ago?" At another point, he turned to Bermudez and asked, "Do you understand why Chris is so frustrated?" What is important to note here is that there were no similar questions directed at Simcox by Hook. Simcox was not asked whether or not he could understand the frustration of Bermudez and others. The clear presumption here is that undocumented migrants would be an understandable source of frustration. The possibility that the circumstances motivating migrants to come to the United States without documents to live and work and attempt to carry on with life might also be quite frustrating—or that those who understood this issue from Simcox's perspective might be a source of frustration—was not broached. In addition, while Hook considered it relevant to bring in Bermudez's background as an undocumented migrant and thus as someone who had broken the law, he saw no corresponding relevance to broach the subject of Simcox's previous weapons charges, which were also a case of breaking of the law. The resulting representation played into the legality/illegality framing that is so prevalent and that connects migrants with either current or past illegality, while ignoring such situations as Simcox's, whose quite recent actions were also illegal. Simcox was portrayed as the good citizen frustrated with his government's failure to uphold the law and with migrants continuing to come to the United States without authorization. Bermudez and those he represented were portrayed as causes of the problem.

The above examples are not terribly surprising, given Fox's reputation for extreme conservatism. However, we find similar portrayals on more liberal cable TV channels such as CNN. *Lou Dobbs Tonight* is one of the most widely watched programs on CNN and, perhaps more than any other television outlet, it has served to disseminate the anti-immigrant message. From March 2005 through March 2007, Chris Simcox appeared on this program eighteen times; Jim Gilchrist appear twenty-two times.[17] Marc Cooper, contributing editor to the *Nation,* suggests that during the run-up to the 2005 Minuteman border operation, Dobbs gave the organization "millions in free publicity, plugging it for weeks and turning over large segments of his air time to directly promoting the project."[18] On the April 4, 2005, show, correspondent Casey Wian reported from the border town of Naco, Arizona. Dobbs repeated the description of the Minutemen as "this country's biggest neighborhood watch project ever."[19] On April 14, 2005, Dobb's program stated that the "invasion of illegal aliens" was bringing in highly contagious diseases that had been eradicated in the United States.[20] During a discussion on immigration during Dobbs' December 9, 2005, program, he announced, "I support the Minuteman Project and the fine Americans who make it up in all they've accomplished, fully, relentlessly, and proudly."[21] On May 23, 2006, Casey Wian referred to a state visit to the United States by Mexican President Vicente Fox as a "Mexican military incursion" and "the Vicente Fox Aztlan tour."[22] As Wian spoke, a map of the United States appeared on the screen with the heading "Aztlan" across the top, highlighting the seven southwestern states that advocates of reconquista theory believe are being claimed by Mexico as part of the greater Aztlan. Proponents of this theory include Jim Gilchrist, Glenn Spencer, and Tom Tancredo. To the great embarrassment of CNN, the source of the map was the Council of Conservative Citizens.[23] Dobbs' program has also served to publicize writings of those like Pat Buchanan who articulate, often in very blatant terms, many of the ideas that underpin the anti-immigrant movement in general.

Fairness and Accuracy in Reporting point out other examples of CNN reporting that provide a rather unbalanced representation of immigration issues in various ways. On April 19, 2006, Jack Cafferty reported on the nationwide pro-immigration marches, saying "Once again, the streets of our country were taken over today by people who don't belong here . . ." and suggesting that the government should "pull the buses up and start asking these people to show their green cards . . . and the ones that don't have them, put them on the buses and send them home."[24]

## Talk Radio

Conservative talk radio has vociferously embraced the anti-immigrant message, often vilifying migrants and suggesting extreme courses of action. From April 23 to April 28, 2005, the Federation for American Immigration Reform (FAIR), along with San Diego talk radio host Roger Hedgecock, sponsored a national grassroots lobbying campaign called "Hold Their Feet to the Fire."[25] In addition to Hedgecock, nineteen other talk show hosts brought their stations to the event, broadcasting live to listeners around the country from states including Arizona, Arkansas, Idaho, Montana, New Mexico, Ohio, Pennsylvania, Tennessee, Texas, and Washington.[26] This has since become an annual event, with the 2007 forum running for four days from April 23 to 25.[27] Thirty-four radio hosts from across the United States attended in 2007 and broadcast from FAIR's media headquarters near Capitol Hill. These shows were able to reach listeners on 193 radio stations because several of the hosts were nationally syndicated.[28] Their main rallying cry was "no amnesty."[29] In addition to the radio hosts, guests included representatives from the Minuteman Civil Defense Corps, Mothers Against Illegal Aliens, and other well-known anti-immigrant groups. Congressmen Tom Tancredo and Duncan Hunter, a Republican from California, were also featured speakers. Media coverage of the event included stories by MSNBC, CNN's Lou Dobbs, Fox News, the *Washington Post*, the *Los Angeles Times*, and the *New York Times*.[30]

This annual event highlights one of the important vehicles for spreading the general anti-immigrant message: talk radio. Both Chris Simcox and Jim Gilchrist make use of talk radio. Simcox's show airs on KKNT AM 960 in Phoenix on Sunday evenings from 7 to 9 p.m. Gilchrist's program is on the Minuteman Radio Network, which is broadcast on KLAV 1230 AM from Las Vegas on Tuesdays from 7 to 9 p.m. and is hosted by Steve Eichler, executive director of the Minuteman Project. There are numerous other radio programs that focus on immigration. *Political Cesspool* is a Tennessee-based radio show that often features white supremacists. Both Simcox and Gilchrist have appeared on the program. Phoenix talk radio host Bruce Jacobs devotes much of his program to talk of the immigrant "invasion." When crosses in memory of migrants who died in the desert were displayed at a pro-migrant rally in Phoenix on Labor Day, 2006, Jacobs objected, saying: "Whites didn't kill these people, America didn't kill these people. They killed themselves."[31]

Jacobs's statement is rather mild compared with some of the other talk, which has gotten pretty ugly. On April 27, 2006, an anti-immigrant "Demagnetize America" town hall meeting was held in Franklin, Tennessee, and was broadcast on SuperTalk 99.7 WTN. At this meeting, FAIR's national field director, Susan Tully, explained how Border Patrol agents after fingerprinting and checking FBI records would return apprehended undocumented migrants to Mexico. She claimed that a Border Patrol agent had told her this could happen as many as seven times. According to the transcripts, Tully said:

"I said, 'What do you do on the eighth time?' "

Before she answered, radio host Phil Valentine said, "Shoot him." Tully chuckled and the audience cheered.[32] On the program, Valentine also read a personal statement from Tom Tancredo and Jim Gilchrist.[33] The previous month, Phoenix, Arizona, talk show host Brian James suggested on air that a solution to the immigration problem in Arizona would be to kill undocumented immigrants as they cross the border.[34]

In March 2007, a New Jersey radio program on 101.5 FM started "Operation Rat a Rat/La Cucha Gotcha," a listener participation game that encouraged listeners to report suspected undocumented migrants to immigration authorities. The show's hosts, Craig Carton and Ray Rossi ("the Jersey Guys"), began the segment with mariachi music and set the campaign to end on May 5—Cinco de Mayo.[35] The radio hosts have refused to apologize for the program.

While I am certainly not suggesting that the anti-immigrant movement or border vigilantes wholly advocate for the killing of undocumented migrants, these incidents illustrate that talk radio has become a venue for the anti-immigrant message that at times promotes extremism and outright violence against undocumented migrants.

## Internet

The Internet has been a key tool for border vigilante and anti-immigrant groups. "If I didn't have the Internet, the Minuteman Project probably wouldn't have happened," said Jim Gilchrist.[36] As Gilchrist's comment suggests, the Internet is used to recruit supporters for border actions, but also to spread the messages of the various anti-immigrant groups and to facilitate linkages among the groups. Wayne Cornelius, director of the University of San Diego's Center for Comparative Immigration Studies, says: "There is no question that Internet technology has been central to recruiting supporters and disseminating their message."[37] The Internet facilitates the creation of a broader constituency by disseminating news, opinions, and publicizing anti-immigrant events and activities. "These border groups . . . a lot of these people sit at their house and surf on-line and they get all fired up, but they have no outlet and so when they find . . . that's why in Arizona we have people from Connecticut, Alaska, New Mexico, Nevada, Michigan, all over the nation coming here because they're reading about it and they're getting upset. So, this is how they feed their hunger."[38]

Internet linkages amongst the various groups often make up what looks like a complicated web. For example, the homepage of Chris Simcox's Minuteman Civil Defense Corps contains a "links" page and a "partners" page. The links page includes, amongst others, CNN's Lou Dobbs, 9/11 Families for a Secure America, and DesertVisions, a site that contains a series of slides of various border areas. Another of the Web sites referenced on MCDC's links page is the Alamo Alliance, which in turn links to twenty-nine other sites, including the Minuteman Project, American Border Patrol, Mothers Against Illegal Aliens, Las Vegas Minutemen, NumbersUSA, VDARE, the Federation for American Immigration Reform, and the Center for Immigration Studies.[39] The Minuteman Project Web site links to twenty-one of its chapters and fourteen supporting organizations, including Glenn Spencer's American Patrol and Pat Buchanan's official Web site. The activities of the MCDC and the Minuteman Project are publicized on numerous other sites.

Anti-immigrant events are routinely advertised on white supremacist Web sites and blogs. The white nationalist American Renaissance advertised the MCDC April 2006 border watch, as did Stormfront.[40] In response to the immigration reform march of May 1, 2007, in Phoenix, Arizona, several anti-immigrant groups staged a counter-protest on the lawn of the Arizona Capitol House grounds. The event was posted on the homepage of the MCDC, as well as on newsaxom.com, which is something like a MySpace for white nationalists.[41] The counter-protest was attended by representatives of the MCDC including Phoenix chapter president Don Goldwater and Randy Pullen, leader of the state Republican party. The announcement on newsaxon.com stated, "If you're a WHITE person concerned about the immigration issue in Arizona, and in Phoenix, that day, this is a GREAT event to attend." This message was also posted on Stormfront, the leading white supremacist blog.[42] The Web site www.immigrationbuzz.com goes further to post a calendar listing numerous anti-immigrant events nationwide. The Minuteman Civil Defense Corps lists as one of its partners GOPUSA, whose mission is to "spread the conservative message throughout America."[43] A February 22, 2007, article posted on its Web site repeated the assertion made by Family Security Matters that "illegal aliens are killing more Americans than the war in Iraq," citing Mike Cutler, a fellow at the Center for Immigration Studies.[44]

There are numerous other groups with Web sites that publicize border events. United for Sovereign America was started by Phoenix auto dealership owner Rusty Childress. This group's Web site promotes Chris Simcox's radio program as well as Gilchrist's, and it advertises local and national anti-immigrant events. At his auto mall, Childress holds weekly town hall meetings whose declared purpose is to "unite to fight illegal immigration."[45] Childress recently started a "meetup" group to attract more supporters for his organization. Another Internet group that is actively spreading the anti-immigrant message is Grassfire.org, which claims one million members and recently began running "Where's The Fence" television ads, which feature three elderly women searching for the border fence that Congress has promised to build. The group expects this ad to reach fifteen million people in its first week. It was aired nationally by Fox News and CNN and regionally in seven states that Grassfire identified as contributing key votes for the latest immigration bill.[46]

Another way in which the Internet is used by anti-immigrant groups to advertise themselves and to spread their messages is through slogans posted to the bottoms of online news articles. For example, on April 8, 2007, the *Arizona Republic* published an article entitled "Migrant Crime Numbers Proportionate to Population," which reported that records of the Maricopa County Attorney's Office suggested that neither Mexican nationals nor undocumented migrants were over-represented in felony prosecutions or incarcerated disproportionately, thus refuting the popular myth that immigration and especially undocumented immigration is positively related to crime.[47] At the bottom of the online version of this article, the Federation for American Immigration Reform posted the following: "Say No to Amnesty. No Retreat on Border Security. No Surrender. Close the Border," along with the address of their Web site, www.fairus.org. At the bottom of an April 20, 2007 article on migrant detentions, the Minuteman Civil Defense Corps purchased advertisement space from Google for the following message: "Minuteman Border Fence—Chris Simcox to President Bush Build a Fence of U.S. Citizens Will," along with the group's Web site address, www.MinutemanBorder Fence.com."[48]

A search on Google for the more well-known border groups and individuals yields numerous responses. For example, a search for "Chris Simcox" returns 117,000 results; "MCDC," 127,000 results; "Minuteman

Project," 869,000 results; "Glenn Spencer," 1,270,000 results; and "Federation for American Immigration Control," 971,000 results.[49] Of course, these are just numbers whose meaning is not transparent. They do, however, indicate a certain degree of "reach" that these groups possess.

FAIR's latest attempt to broaden their constituency is a presence on the interactive Web site MySpace. Their announcement of this states that "new technologies provide us with new tools to reach targeted groups, like youth."[50] Recently, Gilchrist's Minuteman Project began an initiative called FAXDC, which prepares fax letters to be sent to U.S. congressmen. Members wishing to send a "FAX" simply order a "HOT fax blast" through the Minuteman Project site and it is delivered.[51] The Internet also facilitates what some have called "virtual vigilantism," in which informants can report business owners who hire undocumented migrants. WeHireAliens.com is a Web site operated by FIRE Coalition, an anti-immigrant citizen group. The Web site maintains a database of employers that are suspected of hiring undocumented migrants and has a list of instructions on how to report them to various law enforcement agencies.[52] As noted in chapter 3, the Center for Immigration Studies also maintains such a database.

## Newspapers

> "The Miracle on the Southwest Border: Illegal Immigration Smashed—a Direct Field Report on the Arizona-Mexico No-Man's Land."[53]

The reporting of news is not a simple, straightforward, or neutral enterprise. Neither the selection of stories deemed relevant, nor the ways in which those stories and the people involved are portrayed—nor the headlines used to call attention to the stories—are without bias and effect, even if these things are unintended. The above headline illustrates this in a rather blatant way, and while many news headlines and stories are a little more subtle, they are not necessarily less significant in terms of their implication in the creation of political spectacles. For example, Marc Cooper suggests that many media outlets perpetuated the Minuteman claim that huge numbers of volunteers had come to southeastern Arizona, citing as an example a *Los Angeles Times* headline, "They Came By the Hundreds," which appeared on the first day of the 2005 border watch. The body of the article reports that volunteers numbered two hundred or less.[54] On April 26, 2005, *Yahoo! News* ran a story by Georgie Anne Geyer, "Minutemen Project Backs Up an Overextended Border Patrol." Geyer reported that the Minutemen "volunteers have patrolled the border—not as 'vigilantes' who could arrest people but as a 'citizens' neighborhood watch group.'"[55] Govexec.com, in its daily briefing on April 28, 2005, printed an article that claimed, "After demonstrating in Arizona that a presence of people along the border can curb illegal immigration, border-control proponents came to Washington to try to win over the minds—and money—of the federal government." Statements such as these perpetuate both the idea of the benign nature of the Minuteman Project as well as its effectiveness.[56]

Sometimes an article's title itself involves a particular representation of those involved and the "reality" they face. On May 9, 2005, the *San Francisco Chronicle* ran a story titled "Minutemen do the dirty work that 'government won't do.'" The article states: "Much of the hysteria about gun-toting vigilantes is much ado about nothing." And: "They appear more like a Neighborhood Watch group or a bird-watching excursion than a violent, paramilitary force."[57] The article also reports that the U.S. Border Patrol says migrant apprehensions last month in the corridor where the Minutemen were posted were down by 65 percent from the same period a year ago.[58] It is important to note here how this implies a link between the Minuteman presence and decreased apprehensions, without relaying the alternative explanation—which was the Border Patrol's own. It also fails to explore the more complicated issue that decreased apprehensions are equally likely to indicate that crossers are simply going to other areas to cross, such as to the deadly West Desert Corridor.[59]

Yet another example of a revealing title appears with an editorial published in the *Arizona Republic* on April 2, 2005—only the second day of the 2005 Minuteman border operation. The headline reads, "Maybe They're Nuts but Minutemen Have Been Effective," and goes on to argue that "they have done what politicians and policymakers in this part of the country have been unable to do. They have, as advertisers like to say, reached their target audience."[60] While the editorial does point to concerns about the Minutemen with statements such as, "if the California accountant who organized it can keep his volunteers under control, and that's a big if," it functions to present an overall positive picture of the

Minutemen and what they are doing, suggesting that they have done an important service to society.[61]

On May 2, 2005, the *Christian Science Monitor* reported on the Minuteman Project with the following headline and subheading: "What 'Minuteman' Vigil Accomplished—A volunteer network's effort to close part of border slowed illegal immigration—in one small area."[62] The story begins by relaying the experiences of Minuteman volunteer Joe McCutchen, who spent three weeks in April 2005 patrolling the U.S.-Mexico border. McCutchen "spent 14 days in a folding chair, buffeted by wind storms, face-cutting sand, freezing cold, and scorching sun."[63] He is described as a "retired pilot." A picture is presented of a selfless, dedicated citizen who sacrifices his time and money for this "volunteer network," and whose experiences with the Minutemen have given him a "new sense of compassion for the illegals who are being exploited by both countries."[64] What this article failed to note was McCutchen's association with the white supremacist Council of Conservative Citizens (C of CC). McCutchen denies being a member of this group but admits speaking at an anti-immigration forum in North Carolina held by the C of CC.[65] On January 25, 2005, the Southern Poverty Law Center published a photo of McCutchen with C of CC member Virginia Aberbathy and Wayne Lutton.[66] MSNBC also ran a story on June 10, 2005 from Tombstone, Arizona, which was at the time the headquarters of the Minuteman Project. The story quoted McCutchen: "We've become a third world dumping ground. No society can sustain somewhere between three and four million immigrants a year, half of which are illegal. And we're losing our language, which is the cement of any culture or society."[67]

These two instances illustrate the more general phenomenon that simply "reporting the facts" can become complicit in the construction of a particular reality. McCutchen is presented as a "constitutional conservative," "a 73 year old pharmacist from Fort Smith, Arkansas," "a pilot that will fly one of the 16 planes the Minuteman Project has at its disposal."[68] His assertions that "we're losing our language," that "no society can sustain somewhere between three and four million immigrants a year, half of which are illegal," are presented with no counter-argument or presentation of additional relevant facts. Instead, it is reported that the "language factor and the drain on public resources sounded time and time again among participants."[69] The point is not that MSNBC is misquoting anyone. There is no dispute that concerns about the language factor and the public resource issue were articulated by participants. So this news article is in one sense "just reporting." However, "just reporting," in the absence of background information, can become *uncritically* reporting, thus contributing to a particular definition of problems and portrayals of those involved.

Another example of this type of bias spread by the news can be found in the widespread reporting of estimates of twelve million "illegal immigrants" currently existing in the United States. Major newspapers based their reporting of this statistic on a study by Jeffrey Passel of the Pew Hispanic Center. However, most newspapers neglected to include the fact, as stated in the report, that "some migrants in this estimate have legal authorization to live and work in the United States on a temporary basis. . . . Together they may account for as much as 10 percent of the estimate."[70] The twelve-million figure has been widely reported through such outlets as the *San Francisco Chronicle*, the Associated Press, Reuters, the *Washington Post*, the *Los Angeles Times*, and National Public Radio's *All Things Considered*.[71] The consequences of this, however unintentional, are to present a relatively simple "black and white" picture of the immigration issue. Status becomes one of legal versus illegal, obscuring the extremely complicated nature of the status of many migrants and their families, which include mixed families, those with legally recognized claims to eventual lawful permanent residence status, and those with temporary protected status.[72] Simplification functions to perpetuate the theme of illegality and the undocumented migrant as an alien intruder who rightfully does not belong here. These are the same messages given by border vigilantes and anti-immigrant activists.

## Other Venues

The past few years have witnessed a virtual proliferation of anti-immigrant books. Pat Buchanan's *State of Emergency: The Third World Invasion and Conquest of America* was listed on the *Publishers Weekly* bestseller list for five weeks and on *USA Today's* list for six weeks.[73] This book's front flap states, "In this important book, Pat Buchanan reveals that, slowly but surely, the great American Southwest is being reconquered by Mexico." Buchanan has been given forums in several important media outlets, including NBC's *Today* and MSNBC's *Hardball With Chris Matthews*. On

August 22, 2006, Buchanan appeared on *Today* with guest host NBC chief White House correspondent David Gregory. Gregory did not question any of Buchanan's controversial claims, including his assertion that immigration from Mexico, Central America, and the Caribbean was "an invasion, the greatest invasion in history," and "Chicano chauvinists and Mexican agents have made clear their intent to take back through demography and culture what their ancestors lost through war."[74] On August 24, 2006, Buchanan appeared on *Hardball with Chris Matthews*. In his introduction of Buchanan, Matthews announced that *State of Emergency* was "currently number one on Amazon" and "thanks to this show . . . it'll probably stay there."[75] Matthews's only "challenge" to Buchanan was: "How do you stop—let's assume the fact we're stuck with who's here just the way it is. How to you stop the guys coming over tonight?"[76] *Time Magazine* on August 28, 2006, interviewed Buchanan and posed ten questions that provided a forum for his ideas, absent any critical challenge to any of his assertions. Additional support for his claims appeared in other news outlets. For example, the *Charlotte Observer* ran a story on September 2, 2006, titled "The Immigrant Invasion." The story claimed that ". . . Buchanan marshals an array of evidence and arguments that something more sinister is going on: the elites versus the people; radical chic liberalism over wise tradition . . ." This fed into the popular claim made by the Minutemen Civil Defense Corps and the Minuteman Project that political leaders were out of touch with "the people" on immigration and that they (the border vigilantes) represent the true will of the people on this issue.[77]

On August 30, 2006, Buchanan appeared on Fox's *Hannity and Colmes* promoting his book. He said, "I'd like the country I grew up in. It was a good country. I lived in Washington, D.C. 400,000 black folks, 400,000 white folks, in a country 89–90 percent white. I like that country."[78] Not surprisingly, his book is also listed on the recommended reading list of the Federation for American Immigration Reform (FAIR).[79] The Center for Immigration Studies (CIS) sent out an e-mail on September 22, 2006, advertising Buchanan's book. Praising the book, the message contains a review that was posted on Amazon's Web site, which states, "It is essential reading for all Americans."[80] Buchanan (2006: 63) describes Minutemen volunteers as "spotters for the Border Patrol."

Also listed on FAIR's recommended reading list is Jim Gilchrist and Jerome Corsi's *Minutemen: The Battle to Secure America's Borders*, also published in 2006. A search on Google displays 10,700 results. Perhaps even more notably, J.D. Hayworth's *Whatever It Takes* results in 17,300 hits.

Another way in which the anti-immigrant message is spread is through speaking tours. As noted earlier, both Simcox and Gilchrist have participated in numerous public speaking forums, notably on college campuses across the United States. The most publicized of these events was undoubtedly the forum at Columbia University at which there was a confrontation between Jim Gilchrist and students opposed to him. However, this speaking engagement was just one of many. Chris Simcox has spoken at William and Mary College, Penn State, Georgia Tech, Grinnell, Georgetown, and Arizona State University. This is not to suggest, necessarily, that anti-immigrant groups should not be invited to university campuses.[81] It is merely to point out that such speaking engagements do afford another avenue through which their messages can be spread.

The one overarching theme that consistently recurs in the various outlets that have spread the view of anti-immigrant activists is that a crisis exists that threatens the security of the United States. Threats can be conceived of as several types, ranging from threats to cultural integrity and national identity to threats to the physical security of U.S. citizens, all of which illustrate that pronouncements of security threats are not articulated solely by government leaders. The United States is considered to be "under siege." Laws are being flaunted, and thus the respect for laws is diminishing, as is the government's willingness to uphold them. "We" are under siege from "them." "We" are victims of the crisis; "they" are perpetrators. A deeply complex situation involving two historically intertwined countries and peoples is reduced to a black-and-white, illegal-and-legal phenomenon in which certain individuals and groups become "the enemy" and a "state of emergency is declared."

A related theme is that the property rights of U.S. citizens are being eroded or, at a minimum, left unprotected by the state. This is illustrated in widely covered stories of Simcox's call for Bush to declare a national emergency and send the military to the border. It was also a popular theme with groups like Ranch Rescue. The idea is that the individual property rights of ranchers and others near the border are violated by undocumented migrants who walk on their property. This is perhaps ironic, given the fact that Homeland Security issued warnings to landowners that their property may be needed to build the border fence authorized by the Secure Fence Act of 2006.[82] At a broader level, though, we find the notion that the very "property" that constitutes the physical United States is not respected, and therefore the property rights of all U.S. citizens are violated. Undocumented migrants become "criminal trespassers." In contrast to these trespassers, civilian border groups are often portrayed as concerned citizens on a par with a neighborhood watch group, protecting the interests of U.S. citizens under conditions of lawlessness and disorder. Jim Gilchrist now includes the following words at the close of his e-mails, defining his organization: "A multi-ethnic, immigration law enforcement advocacy group, operating within the law to support enforcement of the law, the power of change through the power of peace."[83]

At times, border vigilantes are even portrayed as humanitarians who provide aid to migrants in the desert. In September 2006, the *Arizona Daily Star* reported that the number of border crossing deaths had decreased in the Tucson sector for the first time in six years. Both Robin Hoover of Humane Borders and Glenn Spencer of the American Border Patrol (discussed in chapter 2) are quoted. "A rainy summer that kept some migrants from crossing and made the journey safer for others likely explains it," said Hoover. Spencer remarked, "I'm really delighted that there are fewer deaths on the border."[84] The article describes American Border Patrol as an organization that "uses airplanes and other technology to spot illegal entrants and report them to the Border Patrol." In one respect, this article is simply reporting a fact and quoting explanations by two individuals who are intimately familiar with the U.S.-Mexico border. In another respect, though, it presents Glenn Spencer as someone who is concerned with border deaths on a par with Humane Borders, thus playing into the notion that civilian border-watchers like Simcox and Spencer, while focused on reporting migrants, are just as concerned with migrant deaths as anyone. Recently, the Minuteman Civil Defense Corps has picked up on this idea and attempted to portray itself in such a benign manner. The group's Web page report on one operation, the June 2007 Arizona Muster, describes the life-saving efforts of MCDC volunteers and how they rescued several migrants in the desert.[85] This is not to say that the events they describe did not happen, and it is certainly not to say that members of the MCDC, the Minuteman Project, or any other group would not rescue someone in distress. Rather, it is to highlight that it is quite a stretch to conceive of these groups as humanitarian on a par with groups who have devoted a tremendous amount of time, money, and human effort to saving migrant lives. The stories also ignore the fact that tactics of civilian border patrols, like some tactics of the official Border Patrol, may result in migrants scattering, getting separated from their groups, and becoming lost in the desert, all of which contribute to their eventual demise.

The significance of the media in framing the immigration issue has not gone unnoticed. Frank Sharry, executive director of the National Immigration Forum, suggests that talk radio exploited "an ugly strain of nativism along with a legitimate distrust of government" to kill immigration reform.[86] The power of talk radio and the distortions it spread on the immigration issue led some Democrats in Congress to call for a restoration of the "Fairness Doctrine," which was repealed by President Reagan in 1987.[87]

# 5
# Attrition Through Enforcement: Constructing Enemies in the Contemporary Immigration "Crisis"

Mark Krikorian, executive director of the Center for Immigration Studies, suggested a policy of "attrition through enforcement" as a "third way" to deal with the immigration issue—what he considers a better option than either massive deportation or legalization of the undocumented population of the United States.[1] A "third way" is considered desirable by Krikorian and others not because of any inherent objection to mass deportation but simply because such a course of action is deemed unworkable: "Even a tripling or quadrupling of deportations, necessary as that is, can't be the whole solution."[2] In addition to traditional enforcement at the border, the "third way" strategy entails a "firewall policy" that would "prevent illegals from being able to embed themselves in our society. That would involve denying them access to jobs, identification, housing, and in general making it as difficult as possible for an illegal immigrant to live a normal life."[3] While no overall formal policy exists that has officially declared attrition through enforcement to be the strategy, it has become a de facto way of dealing with undocumented migration in various locales throughout the country as well as at the national level. Cities and towns across the United States have proposed and adopted various local ordinances that are consistent with this strategy. Operations at the federal level are also consistent with attrition through enforcement.

This chapter argues that this de facto enforcement strategy provides a contemporary example of what a society looks like as it becomes structured along the lines of "the exception." As noted in chapter 1, Nazi Germany is the exemplar of a politics of exceptionalism and is certainly one of the most obvious and blatant instances of a society that suspended the rights of certain segments of the population and subjected them to unspeakable, dehumanizing practices. A more recent example of a contemporary practice of exceptionalism noted by scholars and others is the U.S. prison for suspected terrorists in Guantanamo. I certainly do not wish to equate the contemporary situation in the United States with Germany of the 1930s and 1940s. Nor do I wish to compare the United States' immigration situation to the situation in Guantanamo. These two cases are clearly examples of exceptionalism in a somewhat "pure" and blatant form and it could be argued that the contemporary situations faced by many undocumented migrants today are not comparable to these examples. However, this should not diminish the significance of the exceptionalism we witness in the United States today. Exceptionalism can work in less visibly spectacular ways and in a manner rather less severe than Nazi concentration camps or the imprisonment of several hundred uncharged individuals held in detention on the end of an island in the Caribbean.

The less extreme manifestations of exceptionalism should not be dismissed as unimportant. They can and do have devastating effects on the individuals and communities subjected to them. They raise important questions about the depth and breadth of our professed democratic values and about how we attribute worth to human beings with or without documents and citizenship. I argue that the United States is increasingly structured along the lines of the exception in that certain segments of the population are, in various ways, segmented from the general population and denied the rights and protections accorded to the rest of the population. This exceptionalism works its way into people's daily lives, affecting their most basic elements of existence and relationships. It creates a group of people set off from the rest of society, considered "others" and at least potential enemies of the rest of the population. Further, this chapter argues, the border vigilante and anti-immigrant movement is very much implicated in this. By drawing upon the rhetoric of law and order (among other things), border vigilantes have forged important linkages with and have been embraced by the anti-immigrant movement, which has facilitated their legitimacy and added a loud and widely disseminated voice to calls for anti-immigrant measures. Law has become an important tool of this movement. The "attrition through enforcement" strategy coincides perfectly with the kinds of policies promoted by the general anti-immigrant movement, including civilian border control groups. In fact, the complaint of these groups is that not enough effort is being put into this strategy.

This chapter examines several tactics that are part of the "attrition through enforcement" strategy that have been put into practice over the past few years. These can reasonably be connected to the increased focus on undocumented immigration brought on in large part by the overwhelming amount of attention and rather loud support that anti-immigrant voices have received. The proliferation of civilian border patrol groups geographically, in addition to the expansion of their goals and actions into realms of the immigration issue other than the physical patrolling of the U.S.-Mexico border, has been a major factor in the unprecedented grassroots movement against undocumented migrants.[4] Certainly, one should not unduly exaggerate the consequences of civilian border patrol groups. However, we should also be careful not to underestimate their significance. As noted in chapter 1, I am not making the claim that all of the items discussed below have been directly "caused" by these groups in a strict social-scientific sense. There are many actors who are connected in various ways, often simply by shared sentiments, who are implicated in the promotion of heavy-handed immigration enforcement. The point to be stressed is that the proliferation of these groups in recent times is arguably without precedent, and they have functioned to "fan the flames" of anti-immigrant sentiment for ordinary citizens and policy makers alike. In that the 2005 Minuteman Project border watch is considered by those within the anti-immigrant movement to have been an important catalyst in pushing the debate further in their direction, it is reasonable to suggest that border vigilantes are implicated in the overall atmosphere and courses of action that have resulted from this shift.

Another important point made in this chapter is that decisions that are implicated in the politics of exceptionalism are often dispersed and made at numerous levels (such as at the local, state, and national levels) and by numerous individuals. So, the structuring of society along the lines of the exception is not the result of a unified decision from above that comes from what might be considered a single, sovereign entity. Rather, there are many ways in which this structuring takes place that make it virtually impossible to locate a center of decision. The law cannot be said to be the sole prerogative of "the sovereign" because, as this case illustrates, it becomes impossible to pinpoint one entity who makes the decisions that usher in the various forms of exceptionalism we see today revolving around the contemporary immigration "crisis." This chapter is not meant to be an exhaustive, detailed analysis of the practices entailed in the strategy of attrition through enforcement. Instead, it is meant to illustrate the ways in which proposed solutions to the contemporary immigration "crisis" are leading to a structuring of society along lines that are at odds with values of democracy and equal rights—and often with very basic notions of human and civil rights.

## "Taking Back America One Community at A Time"[5]

Recent scholarship suggests the importance of local actions in reconfiguring U.S. immigration policy. Policies formulated at local levels have significantly affected the ways in which immigration is handled. Based on data from the period 1998 to 2003, Wells (2004) suggests that this has resulted in "an affirmation and protection of immigrants' rights at the local level, even as they are being denied and constricted in the nation as a whole." The importance of local-level policies has only increased in the past few years. However, I would argue that the direction of these policies has drastically shifted from protecting migrants at the local level, as Wells suggests, to creating extreme vulnerabilities amongst migrants, especially those who are undocumented. One of the major avenues through which the attrition through enforcement strategy is carried out involves state and local levels in contrast to immigration enforcement at the federal level. As of August 2006, more than half the states in the country had passed immigration measures aimed at denying access to jobs and various benefits to undocumented migrants.[6] According to the Center for New Community, during the six-month period from September 2006 to February 2007 alone, 105 anti-immigrant ordinances were introduced, passed, or considered.[7] The amount of state and local legislation addressing immigration continues to increase. As of April 13, 2007, state legislators in all fifty states had introduced at least 1169 bills and resolutions pertaining to immigration. This is more than twice the 570 bills introduced in 2006.[8] By the fall of 2007, the number had climbed to 1562, representing a 250-percent increase over 2006.[9]

In the past few years, Arizona has come to be considered the epicenter of anti-immigrantism. This is due, in part, to the "Minuteman phenomena" and the passage of Proposition 200, which was a precursor and model for much of the recent state and local-level legislation. In August 2005, another immigration-related law went into effect in Arizona, which gave prosecutors the power to prosecute those who smuggle people across the Arizona border. In March 2006, Maricopa County sheriff's deputies jailed fifty-four migrants on "suspicion of conspiring with a coyote or human smuggler to sneak them into the United States."[10] This was the first time local authorities applied the new law, and it was applied in a way that many defense attorneys say was not intended—that is, they argue that a person cannot smuggle himself and thus cannot be charged with conspiracy.[11]

On May 2, 2006, Maricopa County sheriff Joe Arpaio announced that he would form a posse with one hundred deputies and other volunteers to patrol the desert in Maricopa County in search of undocumented migrants.[12] This represented one of the toughest approaches yet by state and local law enforcement in addressing undocumented immigration. On May 10, the posse went out for the first time, patrolling the desert all night and into the early morning. "We have to do something about illegal immigration," said Sheriff Joe. By 10 p.m., 146 people had been taken into custody.[13] Maricopa County attorney Andrew Thomas issued an opinion saying that undocumented migrants suspected of paying a coyote (smuggler) could be prosecuted as conspirators. By mid-June 2006, Arpaio had arrested enough undocumented migrants that at least eleven more tents at his tent city jail were needed to accommodate them.[14] In October, Adolfo Guzman-Garcia, the first undocumented migrant to be tried under the new anti-smuggling law, was convicted and faced the possibility of four years in jail. Two months later, the conviction was thrown out by Maricopa Superior Court Judge Thomas O'Toole, who said he did not believe there was sufficient evidence that Guzman-Garcia was part of a human smuggling ring.[15] However, this dismissal is not necessarily precedent setting, as human-smuggling cases are considered a new area of law.

Arpaio continues to arrest migrants for smuggling and on April 5, 2007, his office reached a milestone, arresting the five-hundredth undocumented migrant under the state's anti-human-smuggling law.[16] In early 2007, federal authorities negotiated an agreement with Arpaio authorizing sheriff's deputies to double as immigration agents and to verify the immigration status of every person booked into a Maricopa County jail.[17] Arizona is not unique in using local law enforcement to arrest undocumented migrants. As of March 2007, more than sixty law enforcement agencies across the country had teamed up with the federal government so as to have the power to arrest undocumented migrants.[18]

In November 2006, the state of Arizona passed four propositions negatively affecting undocumented migrants. All received more than 70-percent voter approval. Proposition 100 amended the Arizona Constitution to deny bail to undocumented migrants who are charged with class

1, 2, 3, or 4 felonies. In June 2007, the Arizona House tentatively approved a bill that permits a judge to deny bail based on "probable cause" that a defendant is here illegally rather than on the stricter "preponderance of evidence."[19] Proposition 102 denies civil lawsuit awards to anyone who is undocumented. Under this proposition, someone who is undocumented cannot receive punitive damages even if, for example, he or she is hit by a drunk driver. Proposition 103 makes English the official language of the state of Arizona. Finally, Proposition 300 requires undocumented students to pay out-of-state tuition rates at the state's public universities and prohibits them from receiving any type of financial assistance that is funded with state money. Arizona universities are now required to check the legal status of students. This proposition also denies undocumented migrants access to adult literacy programs and other publicly funded social services.[20] Currently, out-of-state undergraduate tuition at Arizona State University is around $15,000 per year compared with an in-state tuition of approximately $4,600. Similarly, Northern Arizona University's out-of-state tuition is $13,000 versus $4,500 for in-state, and the University of Arizona's tuition is $14,000 for out of state versus $4,700 in-state. Clearly, this bill puts college beyond the reach of many students.[21] In addition, undocumented migrants enrolled in adult education classes, including English classes, will be kicked out if they cannot provide the proper documentation.[22]

A few months after these measures were passed, a poll conducted by the Walter Cronkite School and Public TV Channel 8 found that 51 percent of respondents were in favor of classifying undocumented migrants who committed serious crimes as "domestic terrorists," and 65 percent were in favor of charging undocumented migrants with criminal trespassing.[23] In July 2007, Arizona Governor Janet Napolitano signed the Fair and Legal Employment Act, which prohibits employers from knowingly hiring undocumented workers. The law went into effect on January 1, 2008, and will penalize employers who intentionally hire undocumented workers with a permanent loss of their business licenses on the second offense. Representative Russell Pearce, a Republican from Mesa who sponsored the bill, is currently trying to get a citizens' proposal on the 2008 ballot that would revoke a violator's license on a first offense.[24]

Border states are not the only regions enamored with immigration legislation that promotes attrition through enforcement. One of the most well-known local ordinances was passed in Hazleton, Pennsylvania, in July 2006. Mayor Louis Barletta and the Hazleton City Council, in a vote of 4 to 1, passed the "Illegal Immigration Relief Act." The Act makes it illegal to rent to undocumented migrants and imposes a $1000-a-day fine on landlords who do so. It also revokes the business licenses of those who hire undocumented migrants. It declares English the official language and forbids employees to translate documents into another language without official authorization.[25] The ordinance also denies business permits and city contracts to any business that hires or "aids or abets" by any means—"no matter how indirect"—any undocumented immigrant.[26] Almost immediately after passage of this ordinance, a federal lawsuit was filed by the American Civil Liberties Union (ACLU) and the Puerto Rican Legal Defense Fund, on behalf of eleven Hazleton residents and business owners and three non-profits, in an attempt to block the legislation. As of March 2007, enforcement had been barred pending the outcome of the trial.[27]

The trial sparked responses in support of Barletta and the anti-immigration measure. The Minuteman Civil Defense Corps appealed on its Web site for contributions to www.smalltowndefenders.com, a site hosted by Barletta that elicits money for Hazleton's legal fund.[28] Lou Dobbs's "Broken Borders" segment of May 2, 2007, featured a special report on the efforts of Hazleton to combat undocumented immigration. The show's Web site contained a section titled "Town Under Siege," with a link to Small Town Defenders and an address for those wishing to contribute to Hazleton's defense fund.[29] A Ku Klux Klan group also voiced its support for Barletta. A letter was sent to Barletta from Joseph V. Bednarsky Jr., who identified himself as "imperial wizard" of the Confederate Knights of the Ku Klux Klan in Millville, New Jersey.[30]

While Hazleton's ordinance has been blocked from being enforced pending the judge's decision, it is not without consequence. Families began moving out of the city in what some have called a "rapid exodus of as many as 5,000 people."[31] Barletta said, "It's been incredible. We have literally seen people loading up mattresses and furniture and leaving the city en masse. That was our goal."[32] Other cities and municipalities have followed or attempted to follow Hazleton's model. The Mohave County Minutemen asked the city councils of Bullhead City and Kingman, Arizona, to adopt the same ordinance passed by Hazleton. Luca Zanna of the Minutemen said that if every city adopted the ordinance, "the illegals would just go back to where they came from."[33]

Valley Park, Missouri, passed a similar ordinance and became one of the first cities to enforce it. Apartment complex owner James Zhang said that some families living in his Cheryl Lane Apartments, fearing deportation, left so quickly that they did not even take their furniture. The Archdiocese of St. Louis helped relocate more than twenty families.[34] In November 2006, the Dallas suburb Farmers Branch became the first Texas municipality to fine landlords for renting to undocumented migrants. This housing ordinance was passed by the city council in a 6 to 0 vote. Violations are punishable by a $500 fine per tenant per each day of violation. The ordinance states that it is in response to "widespread concern of future terrorist attacks following the events of Sept. 11, 2001."[35] Lawsuits have been filed in both the Valley Park and Farmers Branch cases, as well as in other similar cases. In July 2006, a coalition of landlords and the Metropolitan St. Louis Equal Housing Opportunity Council challenged the Valley Park ordinance. St. Louis Circuit Court Judge Barbara Wallace issued a temporary restraining order to block enforcement.[36] In December 2006, the ACLU, the Mexican American Legal Defense and Education Fund (MALDEF), and other civil rights groups filed a suit on behalf of Farmers Branch residents and landlords. The City Council repealed the housing ordinance, but replaced it with a new one that will go into effect upon voter approval.[37]

In May 2007, Oklahoma passed one of the country's broadest state anti-immigrant laws. The Oklahoma Taxpayer and Citizen Protection Act restricts undocumented migrants' access to all forms of official identification and bars them from receiving any public benefits. It expands the authority of state and local police agencies to enforce federal immigration law and does not allow undocumented migrants to post bail. The Federation for American Immigration Reform considers this law a model for the nation.[38] The law went into effect on November 1, 2007, after a lawsuit failed to stop it.[39] In Colorado, ten bills dealing with immigration became law in 2006 after a special session of the legislature. Provisions include prohibiting local governments from issuing licenses, permits, or similar authorization to undocumented migrants.[40] In Virginia, the House of Delegates approved legislation to strip charities of state and local funding if they help undocumented migrants.[41]

The list goes on and on. It is difficult to keep up with all of the new bills and ordinances proposed and passed. In addition to new legislation aimed at undocumented migrants, changes are often made to existing city ordinances and codes that disproportionately affect migrants. This can take the form of changing the definition of "family" to include blood relatives and restricting the number of unrelated persons who can live in one unit or requiring rental applicants to obtain a renter's license to prove their legal status. According to a report by the Immigration Policy Center, as of March 10, 2007, ordinances aimed at undocumented migrants had been proposed, debated, or adopted in at least 104 cities and counties in 28 states.[42]

"Driving while undocumented" has recently become a risky venture. In March 2007, immigration attorneys in Tucson, Arizona, advised their clients to avoid driving or riding in cars due to the stepped-up enforcement of immigration laws, which often entails detention after routine traffic stops.[43] These attorneys were not being unduly alarmist. On March 15, three high school students were deported to Mexico after police in Gilbert, Arizona, stopped the car they were in for drag racing and called U.S. Immigration and Customs Enforcement (ICE) when the driver did not have an Arizona driver's license.[44] On March 9, 2006, Gilbert police stopped Manuel Espinoza-Vazquez, a twenty-year-old Arizona State University honor student who had lived in the United States since he was a toddler, for making an improper right turn. He had a blood alcohol level of .02, well below the .08 percent legal limit for drunk driving. When he presented a Mexican ID, they called federal immigration officials. He awaits a deportation hearing.[45] On March 29, 2007, Maricopa County sheriff Joe Arpaio introduced his plan to conduct checks on immigration status during traffic stops.[46]

Arizona is not unique in investigating immigration statuses during traffic stops. On January 30, 2007, Hugo Vinicio Hernandez was driving to work at about 5:30 a.m. in Hyattsville, Maryland, when a police officer pulled him over for abruptly changing lanes. The officer ran his name through the FBI-run National Crime Information Center database and found an outstanding 2001 deportation order. Hernandez, who entered the United States through Mexico in 2000, has a common-law wife and two children (aged five years and ten months) who were born in the United States. As a result of this traffic stop, Hernandez was deported.

Disregarding a deportation order is a violation of administrative law, not a violation of criminal law. Still, immigration warrants were added to the FBI database in 2002. Outstanding deportation orders can date back several years and may not always reflect a person's current status.[47] And it is not only drivers who are asked for papers. Maricopa County sheriff's officers now pull over vehicles and check everyone's papers. On September 26, 2007, officers stopped a vehicle in Cave Creek, Arizona, ostensibly for speeding, though no citations were issued. The vehicle was driven by a white man, but his passenger was a Mexican citizen legally in the

United States. The passenger, Manuel Ortega Melendres, produced a U.S. visa, his Mexican federal voter-registration card, and a copy of a permit from the Department of Homeland Security with a stamp showing valid admission into the United States good through November 1, 2007. Still, he was detained for eight hours. A subsequent lawsuit claims that Ortega was the victim of racial profiling.[48]

While the state and local levels have increasingly become realms of immigration legislation and enforcement, action at the national level has intensified as well. The REAL ID Act of 2005 ensures that state driver's licenses will not be issued to undocumented migrants. This act was signed into law by President Bush on May 11, 2005, as part of the Emergency Supplemental Appropriation for Defense, the Global War on Terrorism, and Tsunami Relief, 2005 (HR 1268, PL 109–13).[49] In essence, the Act makes the driver's license a national ID card. After May 11, 2008, federal agencies will not accept a driver's license unless the state that issued it has been certified by the Department of Homeland Security. Other federal level actions are discussed below.

## Raids

Workplace raids, detentions, and deportations have all increased. The widely reported Immigration and Customs Enforcement raids in December 2006 of six Swift & Co. processing plants in six states were not the first or last of recent workplace and non-workplace raids.[50] Headlines about sweeps and raids are becoming rather commonplace. On February 20, 2006, immigration officials conducted an early-morning raid on the Leon family in East Hampton, New York, as well as four other East Hampton houses. They rounded up three dozen undocumented migrants.[51] In an incident in April 2006, ICE agents seized three children off a school bus. ICE officials said the target was the parents, who were concerned about the kids coming home to an empty house.[52] In October 2007, several families from Nassau, Suffolk, and Westchester counties in New York filed a request in U.S. District Court in Manhattan for a temporary restraining order to prevent federal immigration officials from conducting further raids without court-issued search warrants. They also asked that ICE not transfer a detainee to out-of-state facilities without notifying the court and the plaintiff's attorney.[53]

In November 2006, the Southern Poverty Law Center filed a federal lawsuit in the U.S. District Court for the Northern District of Georgia charging U.S. Immigration and Customs Enforcement agents with illegally detaining, searching, and harassing Latinos in southeast Georgia solely because of their appearance. The case involves five U.S. citizens of Mexican descent and a landlord who suffered damage to his rental properties when ICE agents broke into several of his rental trailers looking for undocumented migrants.[54] ICE conducted their series of raids across three counties in Georgia beginning on September 1, 2006, and continuing for several weeks. The raids, which involved dozens of ICE agents, were ostensibly aimed at undocumented migrants who worked at the Crider Corporation poultry plant in Stillmore, but agents also stopped motorists and broke into people's homes. Fifteen-year-old Marie Justeen Mancha, a U.S. citizen, says she was in her bedroom getting ready for school when ICE agents surrounded her home. She saw five men in her living room, one with his hand on his gun holster. Marie's mother, Maria Christina Martinez—also a U.S. citizen—is a plaintiff in the case. The class-action suit seeks compensatory damages for the plaintiffs, but also wants a court order to prevent ICE from conducting similar raids across the country.[55] In November 2007, ICE agents arrested thirty workers who were building a military museum near Fort Benning, Georgia.[56]

On June 6, 2007, beginning at 6 a.m., federal agents raided Fair Haven, a largely Hispanic community in New Haven, Connecticut, arresting thirty-one people. The raid occurred just two days after the Board of Aldermen overwhelmingly approved a plan for municipal identification cards for all residents, including those without documents.[57] New Haven mayor John DeStefano criticized the raids as a "symbolic act of intimidation" against the city's immigrant-friendly ID plan. He claims that ICE made no attempt to work with local police in serving twenty outstanding fugitive warrants on specific individuals. According to DeStefano, ICE agents entered one home with no search warrant and rounded up four men, one woman, and some children. In another home, a father and two children were detained until someone else came home, at which point the father was taken away.[58] Connecticut senators Christopher Dodd and Joseph Lieberman, along with Representative Rosa DeLauro, have written to Homeland Security secretary Michael Chertoff seeking answers regarding procedures used by ICE during the raid and asking if the raid was tied to the city's decision to issue ID cards.[59] Fifteen people face deportation hearings. Their attorneys have filed motions to have the cases dismissed because ICE agents entered homes without search warrants and some people were stopped in the streets based on race or ethnicity.[60] In August 2007, two immigrant advocacy groups, Junta for Progressive Action and Unidad Latina en Acción, filed suit against the

Department of Homeland Security seeking to force the federal agency to release records on how the June 6 raids were coordinated.[61]

Raids in New Bedford, Massachusetts, in March 2007 on the Michael Bianco, Inc. factory resulted in the arrest of 361 undocumented migrants, which was more than 70 percent of the workforce. Most of those arrested were women from Central America. Some were released at the factory, and in subsequent days others were freed, but not before they were taken to detention facilities in Texas and numerous lives were thrown into turmoil.[62] A federal judge has refused to return to Massachusetts more than two hundred of those arrested, saying that Massachusetts has no jurisdiction over the case. Lawyers for the detainees claim that many of the women were either coerced or confused when they voluntarily agreed to waive an appeal for their deportation order.[63]

Most of these raids and numerous others are part of an interior enforcement effort initiated by ICE in May 2006 and dubbed "Operation Return to Sender." While ostensibly aimed at criminals, it has in fact resulted in many "collateral catches"—that is, captures of undocumented migrants who were not targets of ICE but were unfortunate enough to be around when ICE conducted a raid in search of a targeted individual. One example of such a "collateral catch" is the teenager who answered the door in a trailer park outside Columbus, Ohio, to armed ICE agents looking for a thirty-year-old Mexican national who was a known felon. ICE's target was not home, but they grilled the teenager. They determined that he was undocumented and within forty-eight hours, he was on an ICE plane to Texas with dozens of other undocumented migrants.[64] Raids can also result in parents being separated from their citizen children when they are sent to detention facilities—according to the National Council of La Raza and the Urban Institute, at least 13,000 U.S. children have seen one or both parents deported in the past two years due to neighborhood and factory round-ups.[65] In January 2007, the American Friends Service Committee (AFSC) and more than sixty other human rights organizations urged President Bush to issue an executive order declaring an immediate moratorium on community and work-site raids by ICE.[66]

## Detention

Ultimately, many of the above practices result in the detainment of undocumented migrants. Certainly the detention of migrants cannot be solely attributed to the recent wave of anti-immigrant sentiment, since detention has been used at various times throughout U.S. history. Most recently, beginning in the 1980s, the arrival of the Haitian "boat people" and 125,000 Cubans from Mariel led President Reagan to order mass detention. In 1996, Congress passed the Illegal Immigration Reform and Immigrant Responsibility Act, which created mandatory detention without bond for certain categories of immigrants and expanded the number of crimes for which noncitizens could lose their legal status and be deported. This led to a dramatic increase in immigration detention.[67] Recent enforcement efforts and the elimination of "catch and release" have further increased the number of detentions. The American Civil Liberties Union reports that immigration detention is on the rise and that this trend is likely to continue.[68] The number of undocumented migrants currently imprisoned in the United States is a record in excess of 26,000.[69] National detention standards for immigration detainees are set by the Department of Homeland Security in their "Detention Operations Manual," but these are guidelines and do not have the force of law. They are not codified as federal regulations and, according to the ACLU, there is no enforcement mechanism to mandate compliance.[70]

In June 2006, the Customs and Border Protection agency was considering a variety of methods, including the use of out-of-service cruise ships, to accommodate the expected surge in undocumented migrants being detained.[71] During the same month, ground was broken for a 2,000-bed detention center in Raymondville, Texas. Raymondville sold a 53-acre parcel of city parkland for the facility. By February 2007, Raymondville had become the largest immigrant prison camp in the United States. Immigration lawyer Jodi Goodwin from Harlingen, Texas, who represents the immigrants at Raymondville, describes the facility as a series of tents where immigrants are detained for two to five months. The tents have no widows and no partitions or doors to separate the five toilets, showers, and eating areas. Lights are on around the clock.[72]

In January 2007, the inspector general of Homeland Security released a report on immigration detention centers. The report stated that five prisons nationwide had violated federal standards for ensuring the safe and humane custody of suspected undocumented migrants. Specifically, ICE officials and contractors had denied timely medical treatment to migrants, improperly limited access to relatives and lawyers, and failed to disclose and justify disciplinary actions.[73] The report also noted that "the

ICE Detention Standard Grievance Procedures does not provide a process for detainees to report abuse or civil rights violations."[74] Critics of the report claimed that it watered down or ignored the most serious violations, including physical beatings and the mixing of undocumented migrants in administrative custody with criminals.[75]

One of the more disturbing aspects of current detention policies is the detention of children. The U.S. Immigration and Customs Enforcement opened the T. Don Hutto Family Residential Facility in Taylor, Texas, in May 2006. According to ICE, "This state-of-the art facility was designed for families who have been placed in administrative immigration proceedings and was a major component of the Department of Homeland Security's plan to end the 'catch and release' of illegal aliens at the southern border."[76] The center is run by the Corrections Corporation of America and is a converted medium-security prison.[77] At least half of those detained at this facility are children.[78]

The detention of families is relatively new and there is only one other facility in the United States that detains families. Much criticism has been directed at the center by migrant advocates and lawyers. Early in 2007, the American Civil Liberties Union filed a suit against the Department of Homeland Security and ICE on behalf of ten children confined at the T. Don Hutto facility. According to the ACLU, children were required to wear prison clothing and were allowed outdoor recreation for only one hour per day. They were detained in small cells for about eleven to twelve hours per day.[79] On May 7, 2007, the United Nations special investigator on the human rights of migrants was denied access to the T. Don Hutto facility. The visit had been scheduled as part of his three-week fact-finding mission.[80]

## Immigration "Reform"

> "People are at least as smart as goats. Now one of the ways I keep
> those goats in the fence is I electrified them. Once they got popped
> a couple of times, they quit trying to jump."[81]

At least brief mention should be made of recent efforts at immigration "reform." The bills before Congress are in constant flux and opinion is divided on key aspects of nearly every new proposal. These divisions do not always fall into a simple pro- versus anti-immigrant dichotomy. For example, amongst advocacy groups, there is often division as to whether to support a bill that grants pathways to citizenship, however difficult they are, or to support a guest worker program. Some see recent proposals for pathways to citizenship and guest worker programs as better than nothing, better than the status quo. Others regard them as unsatisfactory and short on guarantees for migrant rights. Regardless, it is clear that the anti-immigrant movement has had a significant impact on the possibility of meaningful immigration reform. Randy Johnson, vice president of the U.S. Chamber of Labor, Immigration, and Employee Benefits Issues, says: "They have been very effective in burning the phone lines with calls in opposition to any sort of comprehensive reform."[82] The anti-immigrant movement was active in defeating the DREAM Act (Development, Relief, and Education for Alien Minors Act) in October 2007. This act would have enabled undocumented immigrants who had come to the United States before the age of sixteen to qualify for in-state tuition at state universities. It also would have provided a path to legal status for them, as well as for those who served in the military. The defeat of the act was aided by the misinformation campaigns of anti-immigrant groups such as the Center for Immigration Studies.[83]

At one time in the not-too-distant past, it may have been considered laughable to speak of deploying military troops to the U.S.-Mexico border or building a fence running along the entire border. This is no longer the case. On May 10, 2006, Chris Simcox announced that the Minuteman Civil Defense Corps would start building a border-security fence on private ranchland in southern Arizona unless the White House deployed military reserves or the National Guard to the border and endorsed more secure fencing along the border. On May 15, 2006, President Bush made a prime-time address to announce his plan to deploy six thousand National Guard troops to the border.[84] In September 2006, the Secure Fence Act was passed by Congress and it was signed into law by President Bush in October. This legislation gives the Department of Homeland Security authority to build a 700-mile double-layer fence along the U.S.-Mexico border.[85] The act elicited much disapproval outside of the United States, as well as amongst the Tohono O'odham, whose tribe members span the border. Mexico presented a resolution criticizing the fence to the United Nations Human Rights Council in October.[86] In December 2007, the Bush administration told U.S. landowners along the southern border that it would seize their property if they refused to cooperate with efforts to build the fence. The Department of Homeland Security sent warning letters to approximately 150 landowners from Texas to California who refused to grant them access.[87]

Every immigration proposal that comes forward at the federal level has a massive component that focuses on national security. Bush's call for pathways to citizenship for many undocumented migrants was accompanied by his decision to send National Guard troops to the border. It has become virtually impossible to suggest any reform proposal that does not include border security measures. Even proponents of the latest Senate bill of 2007, which was relatively more immigrant friendly than the House proposal, touted it as part of the war on terrorism and a way to restore the rule of law.[88] Even so, the bill was defeated in June 2007. The *New York Times* reported that its undoing was, to a significant degree, related to the massive conservative grassroots effort that opposed it. The president of conservative group Let Freedom Ring attributes derailment of the bill to "technologically enhanced grass-roots activism" empowered by the Internet and talk radio. Conservative grassroots groups included NumbersUSA, Grassfire.org, and FAIR, among others.[89] NumbersUSA reported that its membership in June 2007 was up 81 percent since January 2007.[90]

These groups focused on the part of the bill whose provisions they labeled "amnesty," and cries against this echoed throughout the country. It ceased to matter if "amnesty" was the correct word to use for these provisions. Facts and accuracy took a back seat to the emotional anti-immigrant sentiments these groups successfully aroused. In Utah, local members of several groups—including the Southern Utah Minuteman Civil Defense Corps—rallied carrying signs and American flags urging the nation to "secure its borders" and reject "amnesty."[91] In Phoenix, over three hundred people marched to the state capitol for tougher immigration laws. One attendee said, "This invasion threatens our world."[92] In South Carolina, members of Council of Conservative Citizens (C of CC) picketed in front of the State House in opposition to "amnesty," with one person carrying a sign that read, "We Are Under Enemy Occupation."[93] Chris Simcox addressed a March for America audience from the Washington Monument, encouraging citizens to oppose "amnesty" legislation. He also met with members of Congress.[94] Some senators who supported the bill, as well as some who were undecided, received threatening messages. Senator Lindsey Graham, a Republican from South Carolina who was one of the bill's architects, reported receiving threatening phone calls and letters. There's racism in this debate, he said. "Nobody likes to talk about it, but a very small percentage of people involved in this debate really have racial and bigoted remarks."[95]

Around the same time and with little national attention, anti-immigrant activist, House Representative from Colorado, and Republican presidential candidate Tom Tancredo sponsored an amendment to the Department of Homeland Security's appropriations bill that withholds federal emergency services funding for "sanctuary cities" that protect undocumented migrants. This amendment was passed by the U.S. House of Representatives.[96]

## Exceptionalism and the Restructuring of Society

The exceptionalism illustrated by practices discussed in this chapter works its way into the everyday lives of those most affected, denying them their human dignity, peace of mind, and security, and often threatening the basic material necessities of life. These effects are not limited to those who lack the proper documents. Rosa and Jose Luis Lechuga are legal residents of the United States who ran a shop in Hazleton, Pennsylvania, that sold mostly to recent immigrants. After the ordinances were introduced in Hazleton in 2006, Luis says, native-born residents began to "look at immigrants as enemies." Business slowed to a trickle and the couple was forced to close their store.[97] Arguably, the "state of exception" inaugurated by the strategies associated with attrition through enforcement is becoming "normal" rather than "exceptional" as immigration raids, deportations, and detention become commonplace occurrences.

In addition to the individual lives of migrants and the communities of which they are a part, exceptionalism permeates social and political fabrics more generally, which in turn affects the overall structuring of society. Human beings are continually differentiated according to criteria presumed by many, but by no means everyone, to be legitimate determinants of who deserves rights and who does not. Society becomes increasingly structured by division, animosity, surveillance, and militarization. The small town of Arivaca, Arizona, knows this only too well. One of nine planned surveillance towers has already been erected on the outskirts of town, about thirteen miles from the U.S-Mexico border. The towers, which are part of Homeland Security's Secure Border Initiative (SBI), along with the twenty-eight-mile virtual fence system (SBINet), are being built by Boeing. They are part of the Border Patrol's strategy of "layering security measures" rather than placing them all along the border.[98] Residents of Arivaca, who have held several protests about the unmanned towers—which contain cameras, radar, and sensors that will send information to Border Patrol agents—feel that the towers are an invasion of their privacy.

The decision on the part of civilian border groups to physically patrol the U.S.-Mexico border is connected to numerous decisions made over the past few years that have resulted in a politics of exceptionalism at local, state, and national levels. These groups are part of an intricate web of organizations and individuals, some closely connected, some connected primarily by sentiment. It would be too much of a stretch to attempt to argue that groups such as the Minuteman Civil Defense Corps, the Minuteman Project, or any of the other numerous border groups discussed in this study have directly caused the specific policies and proposals discussed in this chapter. In one sense, these groups really are the disgruntled fringe I first took them to be in April 2005. In isolation, they—and even the larger, well-established anti-immigrant groups such as NumbersUSA—have little significance.[99] However, the point is that they do not exist in isolation and because of this their ideas, at times considered extremist and fringe, have come to dominate contemporary discussions of immigration. Their voices have been extremely loud and, to a large degree, have drowned out voices suggesting less draconian, more immigrant-friendly policies. One political lobbyist cited recently by *Congressional Quarterly Weekly* suggests that lawmakers in Washington have been overwhelmed by a vocal, single-issue grassroots campaign opposed to any "immigration overhaul that can be tarred as amnesty for immigrants already in the country illegally."[100] The Cronkite-Eight poll, noted elsewhere in this study, showed that 68 percent of Arizona respondents supported giving undocumented migrants a path to citizenship. This position has been overpowered in terms of on-the-ground action by activists and lawmakers such as Mesa, Arizona's Russell Pearce, who described the poll's questions as designed as help "the traitors." Pearce would have rephrased the key question to read, "Do you believe that people should be granted amnesty for breaking our laws?"[101]

In the not-too-distant past, a significant number of scholars and policy makers were touting the diminishing relevance of borders. This is clearly no longer the case. The power to determine the meaning and significance of borders is currently within the purview of a kind of citizen action that has taken a particularly exclusionary form that sometimes borders on hate. This study argues that this has been significant in terms of policies pertaining to immigration. It also has significant implications for the theoretical issues that animate this study. Questions of both state sovereignty and popular sovereignty, as well as security, the friend-enemy distinction, and ultimately decisions on "exceptions" that are made in the name of security are at the heart of the contemporary immigration issue—especially the issue of undocumented immigration —and the responses it has elicited. The material examined in this study illustrates in a very concrete way the elements of sovereignty stressed by Carl Schmitt—that is, the friend-enemy distinction and the practices that put into place states of exception. However, the rise of border vigilantes and their connections to other societal groups also demonstrate that these two aspects of Schmitt's definition of sovereignty are not solely controlled by an official center of sovereignty, such as the state. Rather, the practices that create enemies and decisions that usher in states of exception can originate with widely dispersed, non-state, non-elite actors. The significance of these acts of "statecraft from below" should not be underestimated and indeed can tell us much about the rise of border vigilantism in this particular study. The theoretical aspects of this study also contribute to a more general understanding of vigilantism under other circumstances. The remainder of this chapter elaborates on these theoretical issues and recaps the significance of this study.

The issue of sovereignty has been central to the border vigilante and anti-immigrant movement. Practices engaged in by this movement have highlighted the complexity of the concept of sovereignty, as well as the difficulty of locating sovereignty in one precise central place or figure of authority. Clearly, border vigilante groups have stressed the notion of popular sovereignty in their armed patrolling of the U.S-Mexico border, highlighting what they see as the failure of the state to uphold its own sovereignty. They have trumpeted popular sovereignty in their calls for leaders to answer to "the people" for either not enforcing existing immigration laws or not enacting new and more stringent laws aimed at undocumented migrants. In terms of official policy making, this has raised the question of the location of sovereignty when it comes to making and enforcing immigration law(s). The premise that the federal government alone is permitted to make and enforce the laws pertaining to the sovereign territorial borders of the United States is now being severely tested. For the time being, a federal judge has blocked the "Hazelton laws," discussed earlier, from taking effect, and it remains to be seen if the federal government will be able to maintain itself as the sole "decider" when it comes to immigration. Regardless, not all local laws and ordinances are being questioned in terms of their legality and they have already had significant impacts on immigrant communities, both legal and illegal.

This study also demonstrates the complexity of the concept of "the decision" that ushers in a state of exception. Phoenix's Maricopa County sheriff Joe Arpaio has made numerous decisions that have resulted in his officers going into neighborhoods in search of undocumented migrants. The pastor of one Phoenix church reports that most of his Latino congregation no longer drives to church for fear of being pulled over by one of Sheriff Joe's officers.[102] Arpaio has a fleet of Ford Econoline vans with large red lettering on the sides and rear reading, "HELP SHERRIF [sic] JOE ARPAIO FIGHT ILLEGAL IMMIGRATION & TRAFFICKING. CALL 602.876.4154 WITH ANY INFO TIPS ON ILLEGAL ALIENS." These vans cruise the streets and freeways of Phoenix and the surrounding suburbs. This example underscores the fact that decisions do not necessarily have to come from a sovereign center, but rather can be dispersed throughout numerous levels of government. It also points to the fact that decisions do not have to come from government officials. All members of society are encouraged to make the decision to report whomever they believe to be undocumented. From the highest levels of government to the micro level of "everyday practice," we see decisions made regarding who "the enemy" is, resulting in states of exception being put into place that severely impact the lives of people in numerous communities across the country.

The phenomena of vigilantism receives relatively scant attention in the social sciences. In the academic field of international relations, it garners virtually none. Most international relations scholars would consider it irrelevant to significant global issues of our times. However, this study suggests that the "stuff" of international relations theory can be traced to the smallest, most everyday, and often seemingly insignificant levels. In an important sense, the entire anti-immigrant movement is a manifestation of contemporary vigilantism, and anti-immigrant practices form a complex web underlying some of the most powerful concepts that are significant for theorizing both the domestic and the global political realms. Sovereignty, security, and the nation turn out to be not solely abstract academic concepts about which scholars spend much time and energy contemplating and debating. Rather, they are deeply embedded in everyday practices that function to support the same understandings of the world upon which many theorists depend. Contemporary vigilantes have claimed ownership of these concepts and have put them to work in a particular framing of the immigration issue with immediate and far-reaching consequences.

The friend-enemy distinction is one of these consequences. This essential aspect of Carl Schmitt's conceptualization of sovereignty has also been key in the messages of the anti-immigrant movement as a whole. While for Schmitt, the enemy is "solely the public enemy" because the threat or conflict is between collectivities, this study suggests that in practice it is quite difficult to maintain the distinction between public and private. Many—perhaps most—anti-immigrant activists would claim that they have no personal animosity toward undocumented migrants, that the issue is simply respect for the laws of the United States. As noted in chapter 2, some activists even claim to have sympathy for individual undocumented migrants. So, at one level, Schmitt's theoretical understanding of the public enemy as one who does not need to be hated personally or considered evil holds. However, this understanding cannot be sustained in practice. The widespread dissemination of the idea of undocumented migrants as public enemies of law and order has provided fertile ground for hate that makes no distinction between public and private. The Southern Poverty Law Center has documented a 40-percent increase in hate groups since 2000, an increase the organization attributes largely to the anti-immigrant fervor that has spread throughout the country.[103] A recent study by the Pew Hispanic Center found that Hispanics in the United States are feeling a range of negative consequences from the increased attention to undocumented immigration; two-thirds say that life has been made more difficult for them.[104] Enrique Morones, head of the immigrant-rights group Border Angels, says that he receives hostile e-mails and phone calls regularly.[105]

## Arizona, 2007

The *Tombstone Tumbleweed* office is empty now. In April, a "For Sale" sign was posted in the front yard. An American flag mounted on a pole extending from a support beam waved slowly in the late-morning spring breeze. A Confederate flag flew a few feet away. Chris Simcox sold the paper in 2006 and moved to Scottsdale, Arizona—a relatively wealthy city bordering Phoenix and Tempe. He and his Minuteman Civil Defense Corps are still actively monitoring the U.S.-Mexico border in Arizona and New Mexico. In October 2007, the Young Conservatives of Texas invited Simcox to speak at the University of Texas at San Antonio.[106] In November 2007, he spoke at Belmont University in Nashville, Tennessee. The talk was funded by The Leadership Institute, whose mission is to "recruit, train, and place conservatives in politics, government, and the media."[107] The *Tennessean* reported that students were able to receive convocation credit, a graduation requirement, for attending the talk.[108] Gilchrist and the Minuteman Project remain active as well. In December 2007, Republican presidential frontrunner Mike Huckabee welcomed the endorsement of Gilchrist, describing him as "one of the leading voices in this country trying to bring sanity to an issue that's spiraled."[109]

Players in the anti-immigrant movement have criticized both Simcox and Gilchrist for various reasons over the past couple of years, ranging from financial to leadership to policy issues. Some feel that Simcox has betrayed the movement, though Simcox has a history of contradicting himself and making inconsistent statements depending on the audience. The phenomenon that is the subject of this study, though, is not reducible to one or a few individuals. Individuals such as Simcox, Gilchrist, and the many others who are part of the anti-immigrant movement—both private citizens and policy makers—are merely the bearers of sentiments and ideologies whose force and significance is to be located at the collective level. Individual names and faces may be unknown and/or quickly forgotten, but the phenomenon itself lives on, feeding off powerful sentiments that lurk beneath the surface of our professed values of equality and respect for individual human beings and their rights. This study should alert us to the dangers of reifying concepts both on the part of scholars who would firmly anchor sovereignty in an official, centralized and knowable entity, and also on the part of citizens and policy makers who seek to fix in unambiguous ways concepts that in practice are inherently ambiguous—who seek to draw firm and uncompromising lines between who belongs and who does not, who is deemed to be part of "us" and who is not, who is worthy of rights, opportunities, and human dignity and who is not.

# Notes

## Chapter 1. Fear and Loathing on the U.S.-Mexico Border

1. Roadside billboard on Highway 80 coming into Tombstone, Arizona.

2. Michael C. Williams (2003: 511–531) uses the concept of "image-rhetorics" to suggest that meanings are conveyed by images as well as verbal and written communication. This placement of the two billboards would be an example of such an image rhetoric.

3. The MMP officially began on April 1, 2005, with the commencement of their month-long, much-publicized border patrol operation.

4. Some news items (see Hillary Pate [2005] and Georgie Anne Geyer [2005]) have referred to this man as Grey Deacon. He is referred to as Gary Cole in other reports, such as the *Arizona Daily Star's* "New Mexico Minuteman Project Detects No Illegal Immigrants."

5. Russ Dove is a prominent local anti-immigrant activist who runs both a Web site (Truth in Action) and a local radio show. "Everyone coming across the border is a thief and a robber," he says in the American Civil Liberties Union's documentary *Rights on the Line: Vigilantes at the Border*, produced by the American Friends Service Committee, the American Civil Liberties Union, and Witness (2005).

6. Despite the presence at this gathering—as well as at numerous other anti-immigrant demonstrations I witnessed—of what can only be described as characters from central casting, there exists a diversity of people that are part of these groups. They are diverse in age, in gender, and sometimes in ethnicity, and they include children, Hispanics, and African Americans, though these are clearly in the minority.

7. While the term "illegal immigration" is widespread, one could argue that this terminology is implicated, even if unintentionally so, in the further criminalization of migrants. With this in mind, I use the term "undocumented."

8. Rachel Uranga (2006).

9. Susanne Jonas (2006).

10. See Congressional Research Service (2005).

11. In using the phrase "ease of movement," I do not mean to downplay the extreme and often life-threatening dangers that border crossers frequently encounter in their journeys. I merely mean to recognize, as many others have, that

various features of the world today make crossing borders, with or without authorization, a not uncommon occurrence.

12. Scholars who have brought attention to this include Wayne A. Cornelius (2005) and Antoine Pecoud and Paul de Guchteneire (2006).

13. Susy Buchanan and David Holthouse (2007).

14. This poll was conducted on January 24, 2007 and is available at http://www.azpbs.org/horizon/poll/2007/1-24-07.htm.

15. See Cornelius (2005: 777). This has clearly been the case in Arizona. Republican state legislator from Mesa, Arizona, and Minuteman supporter Russell Pearce has proved to be a formidable force in making undocumented immigration one of the most important and contested issues in the state. See Joseph Lelyveld (2006). In a June 2007 poll conducted by the Walter Cronkite School of Journalism and KAET public television, 68 percent of respondents supported a path to citizenship for undocumented migrants and 65 percent supported a guest worker program. Walter Cronkite School of Journalism and KAET Public Television, Cronkite-Eight Poll, June 26, 2007, http://www.azpbs.org/horizon/poll/2007/6-26-07.htm. Still, these relatively immigrant-friendly positions have not translated into policy at any level.

16. See Saskia Sassen (2005).

17. The "gap hypothesis" is a central organizing theme for the studies in *Controlling Immigration: A Global Perspective*, edited by Cornelius et al. (2004).

18. David Jacobson (1997).

19. See discussion in James F. Hollifield (2000: 137–186).

20. Richard Maxwell Brown (1975: 115–116) suggests that the democratic ideal of popular sovereignty was and remains the most vital to the overall philosophy of vigilantism. The other two major components are self-preservation and the right of revolution.

21. Carl Schmitt's major statements on this include those made in his works *The Concept of the Political* (1996) and *Political Theology: Four Chapters on the Concept of Sovereignty* (1992). A tremendous secondary literature on Schmitt and exceptionalism that crosses many disciplinary divisions now exists. A good place to start is *The Challenge of Carl Schmitt*, edited by Chantal Mouffe (1999). Giorgio Agamaben is also a major theorist of this notion. See *State of Exception* (2003) and *Remnants of Auschwitz: The Witness and the Archive* (2002).

22. An event such as a war would be the most obvious example of the importance of the friend-enemy distinction, but constructions of enemies are also notably present with issues that involve international governance such as that of the International Criminal Court (ICC). For example, the strenuous objections to the ICC on the part of the United States, while not evoking the friend-enemy distinction in any direct way, clearly depended on notions of who was a friend on the one hand and who was a potential enemy on the other. The fear was that relinquishing a portion of U.S. sovereignty to this international

body might result in potential enemies using it to undermine U.S. national interests. Timothy J. Dunn (1996) discusses the significance of an enemy for the emergence of the national security state apparatus.

23. The tremendous amount of literature that is informed by this concept of security has become known as the "Copenhagen School." For original statements, see Ole Waever (1995a and 1995b). Also see Tobias Theiler (2003).

24. It is important to note that the line between violent and nonviolent can be fragile and blurred. Border vigilantes say that they do not engage in acts of violence against migrants. While this may be true in most cases, one can certainly raise the question—which definitely warrants raising—as to what constitutes a violent act. Is holding migrants until the Border Patrol arrives and not letting them leave if they choose a violent act? Is causing a group of migrants to scatter and get lost in the desert an act of violence?

25. One example of this is the banner reading "Protect Americans—Seal the Border," displayed at an anti-immigrant rally at the Mexican Consulate in Phoenix, April 2006. Another is the "Terrorists Love Open Borders" billboards that were displayed on Highway 80 leading into Tombstone in 2005 and at anti-immigrant rallies.

26. Victor Castillo (2007) and Chris Hawley (2005).

27. Quoted in Ray Abrahams (1998: 7). Also see Brown (1975).

28. Examples of overt physical violence would include that of the border group Ranch Rescue and rancher Roger Barnett. See chapter 2 for more details.

29. See Roxanne Lynn Doty (2001).

30. The literature on this is large. I note just a few: David M. Reimers (1998), David H. Bennett (1995), Timothy J. Dunn (1996), and Joseph Nevins (2002).

31. Quoted in Hernan Rozemberg (2005).

32. Quoted in Teresa Watanabe (2007).

## Chapter 2. "I'm Proud to Be a Vigilante. How About You?"

1. Jim Gilchrist to the 150 people assembled at the Garden Grove, California, Women's Club in 2005. Quoted in Martin Wisckol (2005). Also see Center for New Community, *Americans for Legal Immigration (ALI-PAC): Xenophobia, Nativism, and Anti-Immigrant Hysteria* (2005: 4). Gilchrist's view is not necessarily representative of all members of civilian border patrol groups or their supporters. Addressing volunteers on the first day of the official Minuteman Project, April 1, 2005, Tom Tancredo said, "You are not vigilantes: you are heroes, every single one of you." See Marc Cooper, "High Noon on the Border," *The Nation*, June 6, 2005.

2. Stacey O'Connell resigned this post on March 30, 2006, in order to focus on his campaign for a member of the Phoenix City Council. Letter posted on MCDC forum by Stacy O'Connell, http://forum.minutemanhq.comphpBB2/

viewtopic.php?t=4840 (accessed December 1, 2006). Subsequently, O'Connell and several other members of the MCDC broke with Simcox and formed a new group, Patriots' Border Alliance. This group continues to patrol the U.S.-Mexico border and to demonstrate on city streets. See Jerry Seper (2007) and Gentry Braswell (2007).

3. Claudine LoMonaco (2006).

4. Also see O'Connell (2007).

5. Arthur Rotstein (2006).

6. Side arms are small weapons such as pistols and handguns that can be carried in a holster. Long arms have extended barrels and commonly extend to around fifty centimeters or longer.

7. The MCDC operates out of the original ranch house, which the owners have let them use.

8. From a resolution of northern Indiana vigilantes in 1858, quoted in Brown (1975: 95).

9. Chris Simcox, "Enough is Enough," *Tombstone Tumbleweed*, October 24, 2002.

10. Ray Abrahams (1998) calls attention to the variety of places in which vigilantism has appeared as an idea and/or a reality, such as China, South Africa, Britain, El Salvador, and Guatemala.

11. See Brown (1976: 79–109) and D.J. Mulloy (2004).

12. Quoted in Yvonne Abraham (2006).

13. Brown (1975: 104–105).

14. It should be noted that while some ranchers and property owners near the border support border vigilante groups, not all of them do. Some property owners have permitted Humane Borders to erect water stations on their lands and have allowed No More Deaths to set up camps on their property for the purpose of aiding migrants.

15. See quote in LoMonaco (2006). Also see Chris Simcox in the American Civil Liberties Union's film *Rights on the Line: Vigilantes at the Border* (2005). This characterization is consistent with that of earlier vigilante groups. In 1995, before the Senate Judiciary Subcommittee on Terrorism, Technology, and Government Information, John Trochmann and Bob Fletcher of the Militia of Montana characterized the militia movement as a "giant neighborhood watch" standing guard against "oppressive public servants" who were threatening the Constitution. See Mulloy (2004: 145).

16. American Patrol Web site, http://www.americanpatrol.com (accessed October 10, 2006).

17. Mothers Against Illegal Aliens Web site, http://mothersagainstillegal aliens .org (accessed October 10, 2006).

18. April 16, 2005, at the *Tombstone Tumbleweed* office.

19. Quoted in Randy Hall (2007). Gilchrist pointedly uses the phrase "killed

in action" to refer to victims of homicide or manslaughter perpetrated by un-documented migrants.

20. For example, see the Web site of The Dustin Inman Society, http://www .thedustininmansociety.org/no_more_deaths/no_more_deaths.html, which claims that "Illegal aliens murder 12 Americans daily."

OperationBodyCount.com, a project of the FIRE Coalition, maintains a Web site that publicizes its claims that "over 9,000 Americans are killed by illegal aliens every year in the United States." See http://www.firecoalition.com/obc/ (accessed June 22, 2007).

21. The study shows that, in contrast to conventional wisdom, the incarcera-tion rate for native-born males between the ages of eighteen and thirty-nine was four times the rate of foreign-born males within the same age range. See Ruben G. Rumbaut et al. (2007).

22. The Hanigans were tried three times, once locally and twice in federal court. George Hanigan died before the case went to trial, Thomas was acquitted, and Patrick was convicted. See Tom Miller (1992: chapter 12), Bob Moser (spring 2003), and Charles Strum (1982).

23. Susy Buchanan and David Holthouse, "The Franchise," *Southern Poverty Law Center Intelligence Report*, fall 2005; Center for New Community, "Shell Games: The 'Minutemen' and Vigilante Anti-Immigrant Politics" October, 2005. Also see Anti-Defamation League (2003: 1) and Devin Burghart (2005). Not surprisingly, the Ku Klux Klan has a long history of advocating restrictions on immigration. See Reimers (1998: 20).

24. Carlos M. Larralde and Richard Griswold del Castillo (2000).

25. Metzger got 33,000 votes but lost the election. See Susy Buchanan and David Holthouse, "Playing Rough," *Southern Poverty Law Center Intelligence Report*, fall 2005.

26. See Peter Applebome (1986: A15). Civilian Materiel Assistance was an anti-communist, paramilitary organization that had been involved in providing aid to rebels in Nicaragua. Also see Martin Van Der Werf and Keoki Skinner (1986), James H. Maish (1986), and James Coates (1986). Copies of these articles and others are contained in Paul de Armond's report *Racist Origins of Border Militias: The History of White Supremacists* (2006).

27. Yvette De La Garza, Greg Magnus, and Lisa Castro (2003); Franc Contreras (2006); Congressional Research Service (2005); and Daniel Sheehy (2005: 74).

28. Quoted in Patrick J. McDonnell (2001).

29. Congressional Research Service (2005). Proposition 187 was a severe anti-immigrant bill passed in the state of California that, among other things, denied public education, social services, and health care services (with the exception of emergencies) to unauthorized immigrants. It was subsequently declared uncon-stitutional. See Joseph Nevins (2002: 91–92) and David M. Reimers (1998: 20).

30. The year 1994 was also the year that Operation Gatekeeper, as part of the

policy of "prevention through deterrence," was put into effect in San Diego along the U.S.-Mexico border. "Prevention trough deterrence" is a border strategy developed by the Immigration and Naturalization Service (INS) in 1994 in consultation with the U.S. Defense Department's Center for Low Intensity Conflict. The strategy entailed targeting most heavily used undocumented crossing areas, which at the time were San Diego, California, and El Paso, Texas. Operations have been extended to cover large parts of Arizona and New Mexico as well. See Timothy J. Dunn (1996) and Nevins (2002), as well as Sang Kil and Cecilia Menjivar (2006).

31. Quoted in Sheehy (2005: 73). The fence has never been completed, though it now stretches for about twenty-five miles from the Pacific Ocean to the Tecate Mountains. It has been stalled due to lawsuits from environmentalists. Homeland Security Secretary Michael Chertoff authorized completion of the fence after a law was passed by Congress allowing him to waive environmental protection laws. See Agence France Presse (2005). The waiver authority is part of the REAL ID Act of 2005, national security legislation that was tacked onto a military spending bill approved earlier in 2005. The Act permits Homeland Security to exercise the same waiver authority for any future project. See Leslie Berestein (2005).

32. Susy Buchanan and Tom Kim, "The Nativists," *Southern Poverty Law Center Intelligence Report*, winter 2005.

33. Quoted in Bob Moser, "Open Season," *Southern Poverty Law Center Intelligence Report*, spring 2003.

34. Michael Marizco (2005).

35. Congressional Research Service, "Border Security and the Southwest Border: Background, Legislation, and Issues," September 28, 2005, 37. Also see Peter A. Schey (2005).

36. See http://www.americanpatrol.com. In March 2005, the U.S. Border Patrol launched Operation Be Alert, a "community-based" operation "aimed at providing another line of communication between the citizens of Arizona and the Border Patrol." As a part of this operation, five informational billboards were placed along major highway arteries and on all Border Patrol vehicles. "We are looking forward to hearing from the public," said Michael Nicely, chief of the Tucson sector. See Tucson Sector Border Patrol Public Information Office (2005).

37. Southern Poverty Law Center (2001).

38. Anti-Defamation League (2003).

39. Voices of Citizens Together (1996), and quoted in Reimers (1998: 113).

40. Sheehy (2005: 98).

41. Stephen R. Vina, Blas Nunez-Neto, and Alyssa Bartlett Weir (2006).

42. See http://www.americanpatrol.com/links/links.html (accessed November 9, 2005).

43. Bill Hess (2002). Roger Barnett and his brother Don have been accused of using force to detain migrants, though they deny this. Rights group Border Action Network brought a suit again the Barnett brothers, accusing them of impersonating federal agents. See Vina, Nunez-Neto, and Weir (2006: 7).

44. McGirk Douglas (2000).

45. Lesley Clark (2006).

46. Schey (2005).

47. Randal C. Archibold (2006: pA1 and A20). Also e-mail to author from Border Action Network. Border Action Network (2006). Also see Patrick J. Buchanan (2007: 38–43). In January 2007, two paramedics from the Douglas, Arizona, fire department filed a complaint against Roger Barnett for attempting to force his way into their ambulance so he could examine the shoes of an injured undocumented migrant to determine if they matched the footprints he had found previously on his property. See Jonathan Clark (2007).

48. See Roxanne Lynn Doty (2001: 523–543).

49. Bob Moser, "Open Season: As Extremists Peddle Their Anti-Immigrant Rhetoric Along the Troubled Arizona Border, A Storm Gathers," *Southern Poverty Law Center Intelligence Report*, September 2003, 5.

50. See http://www.borderrescue.com.

51. Tim Steller (2002).

52. In August 2005, Leiva and Mancia won their suit against Nethercott and Jack Foote, Ranch Rescue's leader. They were awarded seventy acres of land that belonged to Nethercott. Six months prior to this, they were awarded a judgment of $350,000 and an out-of-court settlement of $100,000 with Texas rancher Joe Sutton, on whose property the detainment had taken place. See Southern Poverty Law Center, "Immigrants Win Arizona Ranch," August 19, 2005.

53. In September 2004, federal agents confronted and arrested Nethercott in a Safeway parking lot in Douglas, Arizona. Jack Foote was arrested a week later on weapons charges, which were later dropped. See Jeremy Levine and Landon Van Soest's film *Walking the Line* (2005).

54. December 10, 2005 in response to author's question at a Phoenix, Arizona, anti-day-labor rally.

55. The *Sierra Vista Herald* reported in 2004 that Ranch Rescue had disbanded its efforts in the Douglas area. See Nate Searing (2004). Border Rescue still maintains a Web site, www.borderrescue.com, and lists a P.O. box in Richardson, Texas.

56. Headline on the Web site of the Minuteman Project calling for volunteers for the April 2005 border operation, http://www.minutemanproject.com/events.html (accessed January 3, 2005).

57. These words of Captain John Parker to his company of Minutemen in 1775 as they faced British troops open the first chapter of Jim Gilchrist and Jerome R. Corsi's *Minutemen: The Battle to Secure America's Borders* (2006).

58. Congressional Research Service (2005). For other stories on and interviews with Chris Simcox, see Dan Baum (2003), Christopher Ketcham (2005), and Robert L. Pela (2005: 7,12).

59. Simcox, quoted in Tom Beal and Ignacio Ibarra (2002).

60. Ibid.

61. Quoted in Center for New Community, "Shell Games" (2005: 4). Original article: *Washington Times*, "Arizona Militia Set to Patrol Border for Illegal Aliens," December 9, 2002.

62. See Center for New Community, "Shell Games" (2005).

63. Quoted in Steven W. Bender (2002: 1153–1178). The issue of using force is not as straightforward as it might initially seem. The 2005 Minuteman Project, Simcox's contemporary MCDC, and Gilchrist's current Minuteman Project all claim not to use force. The question arises as to what constitutes "force." In a film produced by Ray Ibarra of the American Civil Liberties Union, the American Friends Service Committee, and Witness, Chris Simcox is shown with about fifteen migrants in the desert. He shouts at them, "I told you *no más*. Vigilantes get you, man? I win again. I told you go somewhere else, don't come here!" This is not the image of the "new Chris Simcox" that is usually shown in various media outlets. It does raise the question of the right of border vigilantes to hold migrants until authorities come, even if no physical force is used.

64. Jennifer Delson (2005).

65. Open letter from Jim Gilchrist, April 18, 2005. Claims such as Gilchrist's that the Minuteman Project reduced the number of migrant crossings in Cochise County must be taken with a grain of salt. Border Patrol statistics do not support this claim. In addition, crossings in the "west desert" soared. See Michael Marizco, "Migrants Shift Entry to Dangerous West," *Arizona Daily Star*, April 19, 2005.

66. Open letter from Chris Simcox, April 18, 2005, http://www.minuteman project.com/info/letter_cs_2005apir18.html.

67. Jerry Seper, "Minutemen Join New Organization," *Washington Times*, April 20, 2005. The Southern Poverty Law Center reports that Bob Wright was the commander of the first Brigade New Mexico Militia. See the Southern Poverty Law Center's "The Nativists" (2005).

68. Chris Strohm (2005).

69. See Tom Barry, "Immigration Reform Caucus," Right Web Profiles (Silver City, NM: International Relations Center, October 2004), http://www.rightweb .orc-online.org/org/irc.php.

70. Tom Tancredo (2006).

71. Sara Inés Calderón (2005).

72. Anahad O'Connor (2006); Jackie Leatherman (2006); Milliken (2006); Feldman (2006).

73. Witnessed and photographed by author.

74. Conversation with author.

75. Elizabeth White (2006); Alexander Zaitchik (2007).

76. See homepage of the Minuteman Project's Web site, http://www.min utemanproject.com/info/links/html (accessed April 21, 2005).

77. Quoted in Devin Burghart (2005). The original quote is from an interview with Gilchrist conducted by John Earl on June 14, 2005, in Costa Mesa, California; see John Earl (2005).

78. Quoted in Martin Wisckol (2006).

79. Karen Brooks (2005); Jerry Seper (2005); Buchanan and Holthouse, "Locked and Loaded," *The Nation*, August 28, 2006, http://www.thenation.com/docprint.mhtml?i=20060828&S=buchanan (accessed January 18, 2007).

80. Buchanan and Holthouse, ibid.

81. Buchanan and Holthouse, "Playing Rough," *Southern Poverty Law Center Intelligence Report*, fall 2005.

82. Buchanan and Holthouse, "Shoot, Shovel, Shut Up," *Southern Poverty Law Center Intelligence Report*, spring 2007.

83. Rachel Uranga (2006).

84. Ibid. Simcox's group has recently come under fire for not publishing financial statements outlining how donations have been spent. See Tim Gaynor (2006).

85. Buchanan and Holthouse, "Playing Rough," *Southern Poverty Law Center Intelligence Report*, fall 2005.

86. Ibid.

87. Bulletin from Gilchrist printed on the American Border Patrol Web site, http://www.americanpatrol.com/05-features/050719-mmp-needs-aid-campo/m (accessed September 20, 2006).

88. "ABP To Join California Minutemen," http://www.americanpatrol.com/05-features/050621-abp-fobp-ca__/050621__feature.html (accessed September 20, 2006).

89. See http://www.borderguardians.org.

90. Buchanan and Holthouse, "Border Guardians Leader Calls for Violence," *Hispanic News*, April 24, 2006.

91. Ibid.

92. Quoted in Stephen Lemons (2007).

93. See Media Matters, "Savage: 'Burn the Mexican Flag!' " March 31, 2006, http://mediamatters.org/items/printable/20060331008 (accessed March 12, 2007).

94. April 8, 2006, press release, http://www.saveourstate.org/forums/index .php?showtopic=9692.

95. See Buchanan and Holthouse, "Going Lawless: Border Guardian Leader Calls for Violence," *Southern Poverty Law Center Intelligence Report*, April 19, 2006. A copy of the e-mail is available on the Center's Web site, http://www.spl center.org/intel/news/item.jsp?aid=54&pritable=I.

96. Ibid.

97. Morgan Loew, "5i Investigates Follows Up on Lawless and Border Guardians," April 9, 2006. A video of this interview is available at http://www.kpho.com/print/9528678/detail.html.

98. Quoted in David Marino (2006).

99. Stephen Lemons (2007).

100. Kevin Johnson (2007).

101. See http://www.mothersagainstillegalaliens.org/?page_id=61 (accessed September 13, 2006).

102. Arellano was arrested in 2002 during an immigration sweep at O'Hare International Airport, where she had used a false social security number to get a job cleaning planes. She was ordered deported but obtained an extension to stay in order to care for her American-born son who suffers from attention deficit hyperactivity disorder and other health problems. In 2006, her extension was denied by the Office of Immigration and Customs Enforcement. See Kari Lydersen (2006). Arellano was subsequently deported when she left the church in the fall of 2007.

103. See http://www.americanpatrol.com/announcements-ps/az/060422-MexiConsulphx (accessed April 20, 2006). The rally was, in part, support for J.T. Ready's candidacy for a seat on the city council in Mesa, Arizona. As will be discussed in chapter 3, Ready has ties with a white supremacist organization.

104. MIAI Web site, http://www.mothersagainstillegalaliens.org/?page_id=61 (accessed September 13, 2006).

105. Brady McCombs, "Group Says Entrants Adversely Affect Kids," *Arizona Daily Star*, February 19, 2006.

106. Michelle Dallacroce, posted to Mothers Against Illegal Aliens Web site, December 6, 2006, http://www.mothersagainstillegalaliens.org.

107. Shanna Hogan (2006).

108. The written feedback was in the form of responses to a questionnaire that I passed out to participants who were willing to fill it out. I make no claims as to any "scientific" validity to this questionnaire. My purpose was mainly to elicit some feedback that many were reluctant to give me in person. Several reacted to my request with a bit of suspicion, and I had to go to great lengths to explain the fact that they would remain anonymous. Even so, some refused to cooperate.

### Chapter 3. "It's Your Country, Take it Back."

1. Motto of the Wake Up America Foundation: "This organization is dedicated to promoting and preserving our American way of life," http://www.thewakeupamericafoundation.com/000waf-mission.shtml.

2. Quotes are from notes and tape recordings by the author at the conference.

3. The Center for Security Studies describes itself as a "non-profit, non-partisan national security organization that specializes in identifying policies,

actions, and resource needs that are vital to American security." It was founded in 1988. Members of its National Security Advisory Council include several prominent conservatives and members of the Republican Party, such as former U.S. Secretary of Education William Bennett, former Republican Governor of California Pete Wilson, U.S. Senator Jon Kyle, and Alan Keyes. I explore Keyes's connections with Simcox's Minuteman Civil Defense Corps later in this chapter.

4. See http://www.thewakeupamericafoundation.com (accessed November 14, 2005).

5. FAIR and the American Immigration Control Foundation are discussed in more detail below.

6. Christina Almeida (2005).

7. Quoted in Adam Goldman (2005).

8. Leonard Zeskind (2005).

9. T.J. Bonner (2005). It should be noted that the National Border Patrol Council is a union and is not synonymous with the Border Patrol itself. There is by no means a unified opinion on the part of the Border Patrol that the Minutemen were effective at all. In June 2005, a Border Patrol officer from the Tucson sector with whom I was riding expressed the opinion that the Minutemen were unnecessary.

10. Chris Simcox (2005).

11. Some have argued that since April 2005, the Minutemen specifically and the anti-immigrant movement more generally has moved much closer to the mainstream of U.S. politics. See Scott McConnell (2005). Arizona Representative J.D. Hayworth, who stood with the Minutemen in April 2005, said, "These are extraordinary Americans from all walks of life." Quoted in E.J. Montini (2005). It is important to note the possibility that the "mainstream" has also moved closer to the anti-immigrant position.

12. See Nicholas Riccardi (2006).

13. For example, the falling-out between Chris Simcox and Jim Gilchrist is well known. Glenn Spencer of American Border Patrol, discussed in chapter 2, used to support Simcox's Minuteman Civil Defense Corps but now calls the border fence a waste of time and money. See Brady McCombs (2007). In 2007, after a falling-out with Chris Simcox, a group of former MCDC members started the Patriots Border Alliance.

14. At times, the immigration issue has created strange bedfellows. For example, in 1993 Harry Reid (D-NV), along with Richard Shelby (R-AL), proposed the Immigration and Stabilization Act, S. 1351, which would have set a ceiling of 300,000 immigrants per year on all types of immigration, tightened asylum procedures, and speeded up deportation proceedings. Dan Stein of FAIR hailed this as a landmark piece of legislation. The legislation ultimately failed, though anti-immigrant sentiment continued to rise in the 1990s. See David M. Reimers (1998: 132–133). More recently, although Republicans have been pushing the bulk

of anti-immigrant state laws that have proliferated in the past few years, Democrats have also signed on. See Darryl Fears (2006).

15. See Tom Barry, "Immigration Debate: Politics, Ideologies of Anti-Immigration Forces," special report, Americas Program, (Silver City, NM: Interhemispheric Resource Center, June 17, 2005).

16. For example, Diana Hull, president of Californians for Population Stabilization, refers to the "rapidly strengthening and growing national networks of peoples pursuing immigration reduction and a stable population" as "the most important social movement of our time." See "Bucking the Tide Because You Know You Are Right" in Daniel Sheehy's *Fighting Immigration Anarchy: American Patriots Battle to Save the Nation* (2005).

17. See http://www.fairus.org.

18. Quoted in Tom Barry, " 'Common Sense' Immigration Reform: What's FAIR Got do to With It?" America's Program International Relations Center, January 19, 2006, http://www.irc-online.org. According to historian David M. Reimers, FAIR "has become the major force in the new restrictionist movement." See Reimers (1998: 46).

19. The origins of the contemporary anti-immigrant movement have a significant connection to individuals concerned with the environment and population growth. This is not to say that all environmentalists take a restrictionist position. Several groups, such as the National Parks and Conservation Association, Zero Population Growth, and the Sierra Club have been quite reluctant to get involved in the immigration debates. See Barry's "Immigration Debate" (2005) and the Center for New Community's report *Federation for American Immigration Reform* (2004).

20. Anita Huslin (2006); Southern Poverty Law Center, "The Puppeteer," *Southern Poverty Law Center Intelligence Report*, summer 2002.

21. See Reimers (1998: 47). The U.S. English Web site lists only S.I. Hayakawa as its founder and omits any reference to Tanton, though at the time of the creation of this organization, Hayakawa functioned largely in an honorary capacity. See the profile of U.S. English on Right Web, http://www.irc-online.org/rightweb/profile/1557. Also see James Crawford (1996). According to Rob Toonkel, director of communications for U.S. English, S.I. Hayakawa is considered by U.S. English to be its founder, while John Tanton and others helped "lay the groundwork in incorporating and fundraising." E-mail to author, August 21, 2006.

22. See http://www.fairus.org/site/pageserver?pagename=about_aboutmain (accessed August 30, 2006).

23. Anti-Defamation League (2000).

24. Memo to WITAN IV attendees from John Tanton, October 10, 1986. See the Southern Poverty Law Center's Web site at http://www.splcenter.org/intel/intelreport/article.jsp?sid=125&printable=1.

25. See FAIR's "Chicano Nationalism, Revanchism, and the Aztlan Myth" (2005).

26. According to the Americas Program International Relations Center, the Pioneer Fund provided FAIR with $1.2 million in grants from 1985 to 1995, http://rightweb.irc-online.org/profile 1467. Also see the Anti-Defamation League's report *Is FAIR Unfair?* (2000) and "Questions about Source in Immigration Debate," a 1993 press release by Fairness and Accuracy in Reporting (also known as FAIR, but not to be confused with the anti-immigrant FAIR).

27. Southern Poverty Law Center, "News SPLC Report: Nation's Most Prominent Anti-Immigrant Group has History of Hate, Extremism," *Southern Poverty Law Center Intelligence Report*, December 11, 2007, http://www.splcenter.org/news/item.jsp?aid=295&printable=1.

28. According to a report called *Federation for American Immigration Reform*, published by the Center for New Community in November 2004, FAIR gave $11,000 to Voices of Citizens Together (the earlier name of Spencer's groups).

29. The Coalition for the Future American Worker was created by FAIR and the Virginia-based American Immigration Control Foundation. See the Center for New Community's "The Coalition for the Future American Worker" (2004). I discuss the AICF later in this chapter. Dan Stein, executive director of FAIR, is also a member of the coalition, as is Roy Beck of NumbersUSA. See http://www.chriscannon.com/Issues/Immigration/anti-immigration_groups.html.

30. Ibid. Leonard Zeskind reports that in recent years, as FAIR seeks to promote a more mainstream image, it has dropped the Pioneer Fund as a funding source. See Leonard Zeskind's "The New Nativism" (2005).

31. The book is *Any Way You Cut It: Meatpacking and Small-Town America* (1995), edited by Donald Stull, Michael Broadway, and David Griffith.

32. Quoted by FactCheck.org (2004).

33. Ibid.

34. Center for New Community, "The Coalition for the Future American Worker," background brief, January 1, 2004.

35. After Abernathy's ties with the C of CC were exposed, FAIR issued a press release denouncing Protect Arizona Now's new national advisory board. See the Center for New Community's "CNC Replies to FAIR Press Release" (2004).

36. Tom Tancredo referred to Proposition 200 as one of the things responsible for moving the immigration debate in a direction favorable to the anti-immigrant position. Tancredo at Scottsdale Conference November 5, 2005, recorded by author.

37. See Christopher Hayes (2006). Note that the Social Contract Press was the publisher of the booklet passed out by protectAZborder.com at the conference mentioned at the beginning of this chapter.

38. See International Relations Center (2004.

39. See statement from the editors and publishers, November 11, 2003, http://the occidentalquarterly.com/principles.php (accessed August 29, 2006).

40. See Carol M. Swain (2002: 10–11). Also see the Anti-Defamation League's

"Jared Taylor/American Renaissance," http://www.adl.org./learn/ext_us/am ren.asp?xpicked=5&item=amren (accessed August 29, 2006).

41. Quoted in Swain (2002: 232). In an article on Hurricane Katrina, Jared Taylor wrote, "When blacks are left entirely to their own devices, Western Civilization—any kind of civilization—disappears." See Taylor (2005).

42. See http://chooseblackamerica.com.

43. See FAIR's "Black Americans Organize to Fight for Immigration Reform" (2006).

44. See SourceWatch (2006), Brentin Mock's "Smokescreen" (2006: 19–24), and Devin Burghhart's "Black America Chose" (2007).

45. Melissa Nalani Ross (2007). Also see Brentin Mock (2006).

46. See the Southern Poverty Law Center's 2002 article "The Puppeteer." Political Research Associates is an independent, nonprofit research center that challenges the political right and supports progressive movements. The group's Web site, www.publiceye.org, provides a list of anti-immigrant groups and a brief description of the anti-immigrant movement in the United States. The National Immigration Forum, an advocacy group supporting policies that welcome migrants and refugees, also provides information on immigration issues, including policies. See http://www.immigrationforum.org.

47. Media Transparency reports that the Lynde and Harry Bradley Foundation is the country's largest and most influential right-wing foundation. Carthage and Sarah Scaife are both part of the groups of foundations run by Richard Mellon Scaife. See http://www.mediatransparency.org/funderprofile.php?funderID=1 and http://www.pfaw.org/pfaw/general/default.aspx?oid=10843. One scholar suggests that the Center for Immigration Studies often publishes papers suggesting that Islam is prone to extremism and violence and that Muslim immigration is a threat to U.S. security. See C.R. Nagel (2002: 971–987).

48. Quoted in Bob Moser's "Rough Ride: Anti-Immigration Activists Confront a Pro-Migrant Freedom Ride" (2003).

49. See the group's Web site at http://www.cis.org/search.html.

50. Reimers (1998: 47).

51. Stephen Camarota and Mark Krikorian (2005).

52. Phone conversation with public information officer Jose Maheda of the Naco Border Patrol Station, April 20, 2005. Maheda said that the number of calls had increased during April but there was no way to tell if the Minuteman Project was responsible for this increase.

53. Linda Barros and Michelle Waslin (2005).

54. See Tom Barry's "Politics of Class and Corporations" (2005). Also see Mark Krikorian, "Strange Bedfellows," *National Review Online*, http://www.na tionalreview.com/comment/krikorian20040331036.asp.

55. See Barry's "Immigration Debate: Politics, Ideologies of Anti-Immigration Forces" (2005). In February 2005, CIS's Mark Krikorian spoke on the Georgia

Christian Coalition Conference's Immigration Reform Panel. Carlos Lares of the Georgia Association of Latino Elected Officials reported that Kirkorian said that one of the few options regarding undocumented immigration was to "round up all illegal aliens [put] them into boxcars and send them all . . . back to Mexico in the middle of the night." According to Lares, Krikorian lamented that this was not a viable option and would not likely happen. See Carlos Lares (2005). Krikorian writes that massive deportation is unrealistic and promotes a "third way," which he calls "attrition through enforcement." See Mark Krikorian's "A Third Way" (2006). This is discussed in chapter 5.

56. Officially, the American Immigration Control Foundation is a 501(c)3 educational organization. One often encounters references to the AIC, a 501(c)4 lobbying organization. Both are parts of the same organization, which is presided over by John Vinson. E-mail to author from John Vinson, August 22, 2006.

57. See Reimers (1998: 117–119). The Scaife foundations are financed by the Mellon industrial, oil, and banking fortunes and include the Allegheny, the Sarah Scaife, Carthage, and Scaife family foundations. They are big funders of right-wing causes. People for the American Way reports that Richard Mellon Scaife is one of the most influential men behind the right wing today. See http://www.pfaw.org/pfaw/general/default.aspx?oid=10843. Also see Media Transparency's profile of the Sarah Scaife Foundation at http://www.mediatransparency.org/funderprofile.php?funderID=3.

58. See the Southern Poverty Law Center's fall 2001 *Intelligence Report.* Also see Zeskind (2005) and the Center for New Community's "American Immigration Control."

59. See http://www.americanimmigrationcontrol.com/index/htm (accessed August 22, 2006).

60. House Bill 4437 was an extremely restrictionist and controversial immigration bill of 2006, also referred to as the Sensenbrenner Bill after U.S. House Representative Jim Sensenbrenner from Wisconsin's fifth district, who introduced the legislation.

61. See http://www.amerianimmigrationcontrol.com/bubbabait.htm (accessed August 24, 2006) and http://www.fairus.org/pageserver?pagename-leganalysishr 4437 (accessed August 24, 2006).

62. Center for New Community, "The Coalition for the Future American Worker," background brief, January 1, 2004.

63. Zeskind (2005) and Center for New Community, *American Immigration Control,* http://www.newcomm.org.

64. See the AIC homepage for the group's claim to millions of members of all races, http://www.americanimmigrationcontrol.com/inde.htm (accessed August 22, 2006).

65. See "A Statement of Principles of the Council of Conservative Citizens," http://www.cofcc.org/manifest.htm (accessed August 29, 2006).

66. Southern Poverty Law Center, "White Supremacy: Ignoring Its Own Ties, Anti-Immigration Group Denounces White 'Separatist,'" *Southern Poverty Law Center Intelligence Report*, fall 2004, http://www.splcenter.org/ intelreport/artile .jsp?aid=498 (accessed August 30, 2006).

67. See Arum Kundani (2006) and Helen Margetts et al. (2006).

68. The precursor to Vlaams Belang (or Flemish Interest) was Flemish Bloc, which was declared a racist organization by Belgium's Supreme Court. Vlaams Belang was formed in 2004. Its members have a history of espousing racist and anti-Semitic views. See the Anti-Defamation League's "U.S. Anti-Immigrant Groups to Meet with Members of Racist European Party" (2007). Vlaams Belang recently received publicity in Europe as one of the founding members of a political group within the European Parliament called Identity, Tradition, and Sovereignty, which espouses xenophobic and racist views. See the Anti-Defamation League's "Identity, Tradition and Sovereignty: A Who's Who" (2007).

69. Jennifer Ludden, "Supremacist Groups Use Immigration Issue to Recruit Members," *Morning Edition* radio segment, National Public Radio, transcripts from March 6, 2007. The two Belgium members of Vlaams Belang were Filip Dewinter and Frank Vanhecke. Dewinter is a member of the Belgian parliament and Vanhecke is a member of the European parliament. See the Center for New Community's "Vlaams Belang in the USA"(2007).

70. Southern Poverty Law Center, "White Supremacy: Ignoring Its Own Ties, Anti-Immigrant Group Denounces White 'Separatist,'" *Southern Poverty Law Center Intelligence Report*, fall 2004, http://www.splcenter.org/intel/intelreport/ article.jsp?aid=498.

71. Recall from the opening to this chapter that Rick Oltman was one of the speakers at the Scottsdale immigration conference in November 2005.

72. See the Center for New Community's "Federation for American Immigration Reform (FAIR)" (2004).

73. See the PBS *NewsHour* transcript of "Tightening Borders" January 1, 2002, *Online NewsHour*, http://www.pbs.org/newshour/bb/law/jam-june02/immigra tion_1-01.html.

74. See http://www.americanpatrol.com/04-features/041226-man-of-year-2004/041226_.

75. See the April 4, 2006 Minuteman blog, "Field Report: Arizona," http:// minutemanhq.com/b2/index.php/national/2006/w14/.

76. Nakamura (1996).

77. See Congressional Immigration Reform Caucus, "Naco Sector, Arizona U.S.-Mexico Border. A Field Report," May 19, 2005, http://www.house.gov/list/ speech/ga09_norwrrod/minutemanreport.html.

78. See Congressional Immigration Reform Caucus, "Comment from CIRC Members on Minutemen, April 27, 2005, http://tancredo.house.gov/pressers/ 04.27.05%20circ%20mm%20presser.htm (accessed August 24, 2006).

113. See http://www.declarationalliance.us/ (accessed January 23, 2007).

114. It is important to note the distinction between faith-based groups and the religious right. Many of the groups that work tirelessly for migrant rights and to aid undocumented migrants are faith-based but are not part of the Christian right. For example, Humane Borders and No More Deaths are faith based, though religious affiliation is not required to belong to these groups and they are not part of the Christian right. Even amongst Christian right groups and individuals, there is not a unified position on immigration and some are in favor of migrant rights and pathways to citizenship. See Neela Banerjee (2007) and Michael Luo and Laurie Goodstein (2007). Even the National Association of Evangelicals issued a "Resolution on Immigration" in October 2006 that stated, "The National Association of Evangelicals (NAE) is deeply concerned by a growing spirit of hostility toward immigration and refugees who have become residents in our communities." See http://www.nae.net. Also see Natasha Altamirano (2007). Reimers (1998: 143–144) notes that at various times, while polls showed that evangelical Christians were opposed to immigration, the Christian right actually aligned itself with pro-immigrant groups such as the American Civil Liberties Union and the Mexican American Legal Defense and Educational Fund. This was the case in 1995 and 1996 when they were in opposition to the 1996 Illegal Immigrant Reform and Immigrant Responsibility Act. Reimers attributes this to the fact that the Christian right was trying to recruit new members at the time.

115. According to People for the American Way, since the 1990s, the Family Research Council has emerged as a leading conservative think tank that champions "traditional family values." See http://www.pfaw.org/pfaw/general/default.aspx?oid=4211&print=yes (accessed January 23, 2007).

116. Other panelists included Brent A. Wilkes of the League of United Latin American Citizens (LULAC) and the Rev. Samuel Rodriguez Jr. of the National Hispanic Christian Leadership Conference. The attendance of panelists in and of itself does not necessarily indicate anything significant. However, I stress the attendance of Tancredo and Krikorian to call attention to the fact of their repeated presence at immigration conferences and events, which arguably is a reasonable indicator of the "voice" they have been given in representing and disseminating their views on this issue.

117. Jim Kouri (2006). A copy of the pledge is available at this site and at http://www.eagleforum.org/topics/immigration/pdf/washtimes-news-ad-pdf (accessed May 21, 2007). The strategy of attrition through enforcement is discussed in chapter 5.

118. See Alexander Zaitchik, "Christian Nativism," *Southern Poverty Law Center Intelligence Report*, winter 2007, http://www.splcenter.org/intel/intelreport/article.jsp?aid=724&printable=1 (accessed January 20, 2007).

119. See http://www.teamamericapac.org.

120. Charles Hurt (2007); People for the American Way, "Religious Right Groups Join Immigration Debate," January 9, 2007, Right Wing Watch, http://www.rightwingratch.org/2007/01/religious_right_11.html (accessed January 30, 2007); Christian Broadcasting Network, "Evangelical Leaders Get Involved in Immigration Debate," the Brody File, January 5, 2007, http://www.cbn.com/CBN news/82719.aspx?option=print (accessed January 30, 2007).

121. Berkowitz (2007).

122. Right Wing Watch (2007).

123. See Hurt (2007); Berkowitz (2007).

124. Alexander Zaitchik, " 'Christian' Nativism," *Southern Poverty Law Center Intelligence Report,* winter 2007, http://www.splcenter.org/intel/intelrepot/article.jsp?aid=724 (accessed January 20, 2007).

125. Quoted in Zaitchik (2007).

126. Mission Statement of Mothers Against Illegal Aliens, http://www.mothersagainstillegalaliens.org/?page_id=7 (accessed May 20, 2007).

127. http://www.amren.com (accessed May 20, 2007).

128. http://www.kkk.com/bz/ (accessed May 21, 2007).

129. Jim Gilchrist to Alan Colmes in response to Colmes' comment that the Aryan Nation had recruited for the 2005 Minuteman Project, April 6, 2005. See Media Matters, "Minuteman Organizer James Gilchrist defends white supremacists from Alan Colmes: 'Why are you picking on them?' " http://www.medimatters.org/items/printable/200504060003 (accessed May 26, 2005).

130. Sahra Susman (2007).

131. Mary Sanchez (2006); Brad Knickerbocker (2007); Kevin Johnson (2007).

132. See http://www.stormfront.org/forum/showthread.php?t=46007 (accessed May 3, 2006).

133. See posting by "311inAZ," November 12, 2004, http://www.stormfront.org/forum/showthread.phpt=164831&page=1&pp-1 (accessed December 7, 2006).

134. Susan Carroll (2005).

135. See Ben Vinyard (2005).

136. See http://www.whiterevolution.com/mission.shtml (accessed December 9, 2005). White Revolution was founded by Billy Roper after he was expelled from the neo-Nazi National Alliance following a power struggle after the death of the National Alliance's founder, William Pierce. See the Anti-Defamation League's report, *White Revolution/Billy Roper,* http://www.adl.org/learn/ext_us/w_revolution.asp?print=true (accessed January 25, 2007).

137. Jay Gorania (2006).

138. "White Pride Rallies in N.H.," *Portsmouth Herald,* http://archive.seacoastonline.com/news/07172006/nhnews-ph-nh-anti-immigration.html (accessed August 2, 2006).

139. Paul A. Anthony (2006).

140. Carol M. Swain (2002: 16).

141. Swain (2002: 16–17).

142. Swain (2002: 29).

143. Dennis Roddy (2006).

144. Jamie Glazov (2003).

145. Quoted in Max Blumenthal (2006).

146. "White Nationalist Staffs US Immigration Reform PAC," New Community's Building Democracy Initiative, October 29, 2004, http://www.building democracy.org (accessed June 16, 2006).

147. See David S. Wyman, "Former Senior Aide to Pat Buchanan Spoke at Holocaust-Deniers' Meeting," press release, Institute for Holocaust Studies, December 16, 2004, http://www.wymaninstitute.org/press/2004-12-16.php.

148. Amanda J. Crawford (2006). Pearce apologized, claiming he did know what the National Alliance was.

149. Knickerbocker (2007); Anti-Defamation League, "The Ku Klux Klan Today," 2007.

150. Anti-Defamation League, ibid.

151. Ibid.

152. Jessica Coomes (2007).

153. Erin Texeira (2007).

154. Author's interview with Matt Browning, May 5, 2007.

155. J.T. Ready speaking in the American Civil Liberties Union's film *Rights on the Line: Vigilantes at the Border*, a Ray Ibarra film. See http://www.news axon.org.

156. See http://www.nexsaxon.org.

157. See http://www.newsaxon.org/viking_son/gallery/1/ (accessed May 28, 2007).

158. See http://www.newsaxon.org/viking_son (accessed May 28, 2007).

159. Mothers Against Illegal Aliens, press release, May 20, 2007, http://ei dotrne16.com/he/vo.asp?fileID=76702&memberid=133410126&mail=2768102 (accessed May 20, 2007).

160. Reimers (1998); Nevins (2002); David H. Bennett (1995).

161. Quoted in "A Look at the Forces Behind the Anti-Immigrant Movement," an Amy Goodman interview with Max Blumenthal on *Democracy Now*, May 2, 2007; transcript available at http://www.democracynow.org/2007/5/2/a_look_ at_the_forces_behind (accessed May 14, 2007).

## Chapter 4. Spreading the Message

1. Chris Simcox, "Enough is Enough! A Public Call to Arms," *Tombstone Tumbleweed*, October 24, 2002, 1.

2. Mackubin Thomas Owens (2002).

3. Ignacio Ibarra (2002); Miriam Davidson (2002); Jeff Johnson (2002); Julie Watson (2003); Deborah Tedford (2003); Tom Beal and Ignacio Ibarra (2002).

4. Dan Baum (2003).

5. See Daniel Gonzalez, Dennis Wagner, and Susan Carroll (2004: B1).

6. See "The Minuteman Project," November 4, 2004, http://www.frostywool dridge.com/info/minuteman_project.html (accessed January 4, 2007). Frosty Wooldridge is a journalist, writer, and major figure in the anti-immigrant movement. His book, *Immigration's Unarmed Invasion*, was published in 2004 by Author House.

7. David Schwartz and Tim Gaynor (2005); Lara Jakes Jordan (2005).

8. Laura Smith-Spark (2005).

9. Christopher Ketcham (2005).

10. Daniel Kurtz Phelan (2005).

11. Murray Edelman (1988).

12. See "*Hannity and Colmes* Repeatedly Featured Minuteman Project Organizers and Supporters with Almost No Opposing Viewpoint," Media Matters for America, April 19, 2005, http://www.mediamatters.org/items/printable/200504 190005 (accessed April 17, 2007) and transcript of *Hannity & Colmes*, April 8, 2005, http://www.lexis-nexis.com.ezpropxy1.lib.asu.edu/universe/document?_ m=a04e264bf665764 (accessed May 7, 2007 through LexisNexis).

13. *Hannity & Colmes* transcript, April 18, 2006, http:/www.lexis-nexis.com .ezproxy1.lib.asu.edu/universe/document?_m=a04e264bf665764 (accessed April 7, 2007 through LexisNexis). It should be noted that, according to Border Patrol statistics, apprehensions in Cochise County (where the 2005 Minuteman Project operation was held) were 27,906 for the period of April 1 to 14, 2005— compared with 28,505 for the same period in 2004. This is hardly the 94-percent reduction claimed by Gilchrist. See Michael Marizco, "Migrant Shift Entry to Dangerous West," *Arizona Daily Star*, April 19, 2005, http://www.azstarnet.com/ dailystar/printDS/71143.php (accessed April 19, 2005). It is also impossible to verify the number of apprehensions that were due to the Minutemen, as the Border Patrol does not keep track of these calls separately from calls from citizens about border crossers.

14. Ibid.

15. *Hannity & Colmes* transcript, April 26, 2006 (accessed April 7, 2007 through LexisNexis).

16. *Hannity & Colmes* transcript, April 19, 2006 (accessed April 17, 2007 through LexisNexis).

17. These numbers were ascertained through an examination of transcripts from CNN's *Lou Dobbs Tonight*. I would like to thank John E. Dougherty for his research assistance on this.

18. Bill Berkowtiz (2005); Daphne Eviatar (2006).

19. *Lou Dobbs Tonight* transcript, April 4, 2005 (accessed April 17, 2007 through LexisNexis).

20. Quoted in Heidi Beirich (2007).

21. Media Matters, December 12, 2005 (accessed April 17, 2007 through Lexis-Nexis).

22. CNN transcripts, May 23, 2006 (accessed April 19, 2007 through Lexis-Nexis).

23. See "Anti-Immigration Movement Using Hate Group Materials, Dobbs Slams Illegal Immigration," *Southern Poverty Law Center Intelligence Report*, summer 2006, http://www.splcenter.org/intelrepot/article.jsp?aid=639 (accessed April 19, 2007). Executive producer Jim McGinnis told the *Intelligence Report* that the map was provided by a freelance field producer who had searched the Web for Aztlan maps and grabbed the C of CC without knowing the background of the organization. He did not address the equally significant point of the show's endorsement of the reconquista theory.

24. Fairness and Accuracy in Reporting, "CNN's Immigration Problem: Is Dobbs the exception or the rule?" April 24, 2006, http://www.fair.org/index.php?page=28687&printer_friendly=1 (accessed April 20, 2007).

25. Note that Roger Hedgecock is the same person involved in the citizen anti-immigrant border watches in San Diego in the early 1990s. See chapter 2.

26. Susy Buchanan, "Nativism on the Air," *Southern Poverty Law Center Intelligence Report*, winter 2005, http://www.splc.org/itel.intelreport/article.jsp?aid=590&printable=1 (accessed April 25, 2006).

27. See FAIR's Web site for information on this annual event: http://www.fairus.org./site/Page Server?pagename=feettothefire_agenda2007.

28. See FAIR's May 2007 newsletter, www.fairus.org/site/pageserver?pagename=research_may07n102 (accessed May 5, 2007).

29. Pamela Constable (2007); Eunice Moscoso (2007).

30. FAIR Newsletter, June 2007, http://www.fairus.org (accessed June 25, 2007).

31. Joseph Lelyveld (2006).

32. See Center for New Community, "TN Talk Show Host Calls for Shooting of Immigrants," Building Democracy Initiative of the Center for New Community, April 28, 2006, http://bdi.newcomm.org/index2.php?option=comm_content&task=view&id=68Itemid=44 (accessed June 9, 2006).

33. Ibid.

34. Ibid.

35. Andrew Jacobs (2007); Elizabeth Llorente (2007).

36. Quoted in William Finn Bennett (2005).

37. Ibid.

38. Author interview with Matt Browning, Mesa, Arizona, undercover police, April 5, 2007.

39. The Minuteman Civil Defense Corps homepage is http://www.minutemanhq.com.

40. See "Minutemen Announce April Border Campaign," excerpted from an article written by Jerry Seper and published in the *Washington Times*, February 17, 2006, http://www.amren.com/mtnews/archives/2006/02/minutemen_annou.php (accessed January 25, 2007). See posting on Stormfront's forum on

November 12, 2004, by forum member "311inAZ," which announces the planned Minuteman Project for April 2005, http://www.stormfront.org/forum.show thread.php?t=164831&page=1&pp=10 (accessed December 7, 2006).

41. The Web site is now newsaxon.org.

42. See posting by "azshawn" under "special occasion" on http://www .newsaxon.com/events/?action=view__event&id=35 (accessed May 6, 2007) and http://www.stormfront.org/forum/showthread.php/anti-immigration-rally-383711.html (accessed May 8, 2007).

43. See http://www.gopusa.com./company/mission.shtml (accessed June 2, 2007).

44. Jim Brown, "More Americans Killed by Illegal Aliens Than Iraq War, Study Says," GOPUSA, http://www.gopusa.com/news/2007/february/0222__il legals__repotp.shtml (May 20, 2007).

45. See http://www.rustyworld.com and http://immigrationbuzz.com.

46. The targeted states include Arizona, Georgia, Kansas, Mississippi, North Carolina, Texas, and Virginia. See http://grassfire.org/NewsRelease/20070604-266 .htm (accessed June 26, 2007).

47. Michael Kiefer (2007).

48. See "Deputies' ICE Training Results in Migrant Detentions," *Arizona Republic*, online edition, http://www.azcentral.com/news/articles/0420newb1-newsupdate0420.html (accessed April 20, 2007). Advertising on the Internet is, of course, fairly common and is used by numerous groups and businesses. I merely mean to note one of the ways border groups advertise themselves and attract supporters.

49. Author search on April 26, 2007.

50. FAIR May 2005 newsletter.

51. See http://www.faxdc.com. This project is run by Stephen J. Eichler of the Minuteman Project.

52. The group's Web site is http://www.wehirealiens.com/howto/index.asp. See Daniel Gonzalez, "Web Site Targeting Employers of Migrants," *Arizona Republic*, January 11, 2007.

53. Headline from an article written by Congressman Charlie Norwood, (Ninth District, Georgia) and published on the front page of the *Tombstone Tumbleweed*, April 14, 2005.

54. Marc Cooper, "The 15-Second Men," *Los Angeles Times*, May 1, 2005, http://www.latimes.com/news/opinion/sunday/commentary/la-op-minutemen1may01,0,3210562,print.story? (accessed May 3, 2005).

55. Georgie Anne Geyer (2005).

56. Chris Strohm (2005).

57. Andy Asaacson (2005).

58. Ibid.

59. Michael Marizco (April 19, 2005) reports that while the first two weeks of

the April 2005 Minuteman Project saw a slight decrease in apprehensions in Cochise County where the Minutemen were positioned, the numbers of apprehensions in the West Desert Corridor, which includes the Tohono O'odham Nation, actually increased by six thousand. The West Desert Corridor is the part of the Sonoran Desert that extends from Mexico into the state of Arizona, west of Nogales. The terrain includes both inhospitable mountains and flat desert areas, void of water and shelter from the elements.

60. Laurie Roberts (2005).

61. Ibid.

62. Daniel B. Wood (2005).

63. Ibid.

64. Ibid.

65. See Media Matters, "*Christian Science Monitor* failed to note Minuteman Project volunteer's white supremacist ties," May 4, 2005, http://mediamatters .org/items/printable/200505040001 (accessed April 19, 2007).

66. See Southern Poverty Law Center, "Extremist Leads New Arkansas Anti-Immigration Group," January 25, 2005, http://www.splcenter.org/intel/news/ item.jsp?aid=8 (accessed April 19, 2007). See chapter 3 for information on the *Occidental Quarterly* and the Social Contract Press.

67. Brock N. Meeks, "Common Thread Binds Border Volunteers," MSNBC, June 10, 2005, www.msnbc.msn.com//id/7409293/print/1/displaymode/1098/ (accessed April 19, 2007). See chapter 3 for more on Wayne Lutton.

68. Ibid.

69. Ibid.

70. See Saurav Sarkar, "Sidebar: Birth of a Factoid," sidebar to "The False Debate over 'Broken Borders,'" Fairness and Accuracy in Reporting (FAIR), http://www.fair.org/index.php?page=2899 (accessed April 20, 2007). Note: This organization, which goes by the acronym FAIR, should not be confused with the Federation for American Immigration Reform, which goes by the same acronym. Also see original report by Jeffery S. Passel (2005).

71. Sarkar, Ibid.

72. See David Martin (2005). Martin estimates that 1 to 1.5 million people who are generally counted amongst the undocumented population hold current or incipient claims to legal status in the United States.

73. See *Publishers Weekly*, week of October 2, 2006, http://www.publishers weekly.com/index.asp?layout=bestsellerprint&imarketid=1&listdat (accessed April 21, 2007) and *USA Today's* top 150 best-selling books database, http://asp.usa today.com/life/books/booksdatabase/default.aspx (accessed April 21, 2007).

74. Patrick J. Buchanan (2006: 5, 12). Also see Media Matters, "Buchanan Book Featured on *Today*: For Nation to 'Survive,' U.S. Must Keep 'Americans of European Descent' From Becoming 'Minority,'" August 23, 2006, http://media metters.org/items/printable/200608230002 (accessed April 24, 2007).

75. Media Matters, http://mediamatters.org/items/printable/200608250008 (accessed April 24, 2007).

76. Ibid.

77. Tom Ashcraft (2006). It should be noted that Buchanan's book has also received criticism as illustrated in a piece in the *Boston Globe* on September 4, 2006 titled "Xenophobia in Hardcover," which points out that Buchanan "can't resist layering in the toxin of racial animosity, pushing the whole debate to the fringe."

78. Sean Hannity and Alan Colmes, *Hannity & Colmes*, August 30, 2006, transcript 083001cb253.

79. See FAIR's recommended reading list on their Web site, http://www.fairus .org/site/pageserver?pagename=research_recreading (accessed April 24, 2007).

80. E-mail to author on September 22, 2006.

81. It is, however, certainly valid to raise the question as to whether figures like Chris Simcox and Jim Gilchrist are the most qualified, in terms of their breadth of knowledge on the depth and complexity of the immigration issue, to warrant attention from a university audience.

82. The Secure Fence Act of 2006 is discussed in chapter 5.

83. Jim Gilchrist e-mail, "Ex-Official at Agency Guilty of Harboring Illegal Resident." Received by author December 20, 2007.

84. Brady McCombs, "Deaths Drop in Border Sector," *Arizona Daily Star*, September 29, 2006.

85. "New MCDC Team Leads June Arizona Muster—MCDC SRT Save 6 Illegals from Death in Desert," MCDC Web site, http://www.minutemanhq.com/ hq/borderops_25.php (accessed June 26, 2007).

86. Daniel Gonzalez (2007).

87. Ibid. The Fairness Doctrine required broadcasters to present opposing viewpoints on controversial political issues. Also see Alexander Bolton (2007) and Esther J. Cepeda (2007).

## Chapter 5. Attrition Through Enforcement: Constructing Enemies in the Contemporary Immigration "Crisis"

1. Mark Krikorian (2006).

2. Ibid.

3. Ibid.

4. NBC correspondent Dick Gregory used the phrase "unprecedented grass-roots movement" to describe the current sentiment against the relatively more lenient elements in Senate and House immigration bills, such as a guest worker program and paths to citizenship. Dick Gregory (2007).

5. Heading on FireCoalition's Web site, team page. See http://www.firecoali tion.com/fireteams.asp (accessed June 22, 2007).

6. Daniel Gonzalez (2006).

7. Justin Massa and Cecilia Abundis (2007).

8. These figures come from the National Conference of State Legislatures' "Overview of State Legislation Related to Immigration and Immigrants in 2007," http://www.ncsl.org/programs/immig/2007StateLegislationImmigration.html (accessed June 28, 2007). Also see Darryl Fears (2007).

9. Mary Jo Pitzl (2007).

10. Lindsey Collom (2006).

11. Michael Kiefer (2006). Maricopa Superior Court Judge Thomas O'Toole was to decide the case on May 23, 2006.

12. *Arizona Republic* (2006).

13. Channel 12 Local News, Kevin Kennedy, reporter, May 10, 2006; John Pomfret and Sonya Geis (2006).

14. William Hermann (2007).

15. Jahna Berry, "Smuggling Law Gets a Conviction," *Arizona Republic*, January 20, 2006; Jahna Berry, "Human Smuggling Verdict Tossed," *Arizona Republic*, December 6, 2006.

16. Judi Villa, "Arpaio's Migrant Arrests for Smuggling Hit 500," *Arizona Republic*, April 6, 2007.

17. Daniel Gonzalez, "Deputies May Start Arresting Migrants," *Arizona Republic*, January 13, 2007; Daniel Gonzalez, "Officers Get Nod to Train to Enforce Immigration Laws," *Arizona Republic*, February 8, 2007.

18. Oren Dorell and William M. Welch (2007).

19. Daniel Scarpinato (2007).

20. J. P. Wallace (2007); Faye Bowers (2007).

21. Yvonne Wingette (2007).

22. Josh Kelley (2007).

23. Jessica Coomes, "Most in Poll Back Laws Aimed at Illegal Migrants," *Arizona Republic*, February 28, 2007. Information on this poll, along with the questions and results, can be found at http://www.azpbs.org/horizon/poll/2007/2-27-07.htm (accessed June 19, 2007).

24. Sean Holstege (2007); Matthew Benson (2007); Scarpinato (2007); Randal C. Archibold (2007).

25. Michael Powell and Michelle Garcia (2006); Ellen Barry (2006).

26. See People for the American Way (2006).

27. The *Washington Post* reported that U.S. District Court Judge James Munley would likely take months to decide whether Hazleton's crackdown on undocumented migrants is reasonable. See Michael Rubinkam (2007).

28. Minuteman Civil Defense Corps, "Legal Defense Appeal for the City of Hazleton," http://minutemanhq.com/state/read.php?chapter=pa&sid=308 (accessed January 18, 2007).

29. See Media Matters, http://mediamatters.org/items/printable/200705090

007 (accessed June 5, 2007). Media Matters reports that after receiving a letter from the National Institute for Latino Policy, CNN chief executive Jim Walton removed the link to Small Town Defenders.

30. Dick Gregory (2007). In response, Barletta said he had no intention of making contact with Bednarsky.

31. John Keilman (2006).

32. Barry (2006). FAIR reports that on May 15, 2007, Mayor Barletta, a two-term Republican, won his party's primary with 94.4 percent of the vote. See FAIR's news release, "The Mayor Who Put Hazelton on the Map 'Anointed' by Voters for a Third Term," http://www.fairus.org/site/pageserver?pagename=media_release5162007?&printer_friendly=1 (accessed June 25, 2007).

33. Suzanne Adams (2006). The Mohave County Minutemen are inspired by, but not affiliated with, the Minuteman Project.

34. Stephen Deere (2006). Also see Barry (2006).

35. Max Blumenthal (2006).

36. See American Civil Liberties Union, "Anti-Immigrant Ordinances: Valley Park, MO," http://www.aclu.org/immigrants/discrim/27858res20070105.html (accessed June 7, 2007).

37. Ibid.

38. Kim Cobb (2007); Fears (2007).

39. *Economist* (2007).

40. Ibid.

41. Tim Craig (2007).

42. See Massa and Abundis (2007); Jill Esbenshade (2007).

43. Claudine LoMonaco (2007).

44. Gilbert is a suburb of Phoenix. Daniel Gonzalez, "3 Students Deported to Mexico," *Arizona Republic*, March 15, 2007, B1 & B5.

45. Dianna M. Nanez, "'Don't Ask, Don't Tell' Immigration Era Ending," *Arizona Republic*, April 24, 2007.

46. Lindsey Collom (2007).

47. Ibid.

48. Judy Villa, "Migrant Worker Files Civil Suit Against Sheriff Arpaio," *Arizona Republic*, December 13, 2007.

49. See National Conference of State Legislatures, "The History of Federal Requirements for State Issued Driver's Licenses and Identification Cards," http://www.ncsl.org/standcomm/sctran/history_of_dl_reform.htm.

50. Liza Porteus (2006); Julia Preston (2006); Spencer S. Hsu and Krissah Williams (2006).

51. Nina Bernstein (2007).

52. Ibid; Leslie Albrecht (2006).

53. Susana Enriquez (2007).

54. Jenny Jarvie (2006); Southern Poverty Law Center, "SPLC Sues Immigra-

tion Agency," November 1, 2002, htpp://www.splcenter.org/legal/news/article
.jsp?aid=221&site__area=1&printable=1 (accessed November 8, 2006).

55. Ibid.

56. Mary Lou Pickel (2007).

57. Jennifer Medina (2007).

58. Melissa Bailey (2007).

59. Allison Leigh Cowan (2007).

60. Mark Spencer (2007).

61. Associated Press, "Immigrant Advocacy Groups Sue Over New Haven Raids," *Boston Globe*, August 11, 2007.

62. Ibid.

63. *Interactive Investor*, "Massachusetts Judge Refuses to Return Immigrants," May 10, 2007, http://www.iii.co.uk/news/?type=afxnews&article=6098213&format=reformatted&suje (accessed May 22, 2007).

64. Daren Briscoe (2006).

65. Randy Capps et al. (2007). See also Julia Preston, "Immigration Quandary: A Mother Torn from Her Baby," *New York Times*, November 17, 2007.

66. The statement is available at http://www.afsc.org/immigrants-rights/news/groups-call-for-end-to-raids.htm (accessed January 4, 2007).

67. See American Civil Liberties Union of New Jersey (2007). Also see Roxanne Lynn Doty (2003).

68. American Civil Liberties Union of New Jersey, ibid. "Catch and release" involved releasing rather than detaining apprehended undocumented migrants until their deportation hearings.

69. Hsu and Moreno (2007); Center for New Community, "Raymondville: Inside the Largest Immigration Prison Camp in the United States," *Democracy Now*, February 23, 2007, http://www.democracynow.org/article.pl?sid=07/02/23/1536249 (accessed June 14, 2007).

70. American Civil Liberties Union of New Jersey (2007). *The Detention Operations Manual* is available online at http://www.ice.gov/partners/dro/ops manual/index.htm.

71. David Marino (2006).

72. Spencer S. Hsu and Sylvia Moreno (2007).

73. Hsu (2007); Marino (2007).

74. Department of Homeland Security (2006). The facilities examined in this report include: Berks County Prison in Leesport, Pennsylvania; Corrections Corporation of America Facility in San Diego, California; Hudson County Correction Center in Kearney, New Jersey; Krome Service Processing Center in Miami, Florida; and Passaic County Jail in Paterson, New Jersey.

75. Hsu (2007).

76. Department of Homeland Security (2007).

77. Corrections Corporation of America (CCA) is one of the leaders in the

private prison industry in the United States and has been in existence for twenty-four years. Its homepage is http://www.corectionscorp.com. In 2003, the Open Society Institute supported a critical report on CCA by Grassroots Leadership, the Corporate Research Project of Good Jobs First, and Prison Privatisation Report International. The critiques in the report included: failure to provide adequate medical care to prisoners, failure to control violence in its prisons, and substandard conditions resulting in prison uprisings and protests. See Philip Mattera, Mafruza Khan, and Stephen Nathan (2003).

78. According to the *Los Angeles Times*, as of February 2007, the majority of the facilities' 383 inmates were children. See Nicole Gaouette and Miguel Bustillo (2007). In its summer 2007 newsletter, the American Civil Liberties Union reported that two hundred of the four hundred incarcerated were children. See Anthony D. Romero (2007: 4).

79. See American Civil Liberties Union, "ACLU Challenges Prison-Like Conditions at Hutto Detention Center," http://www.aclu.org/immigrants/detention/hutto.html (accessed June 17, 2007). Also see Suzanne Gamboa, "Groups Compare Texas, Pennsylvania Immigrant Facilities to Jails," *USA Today*, February 22, 2007. In February 2007, the Women's Commission for Refugee Women and Children, along with the Lutheran Immigration Refugee Services, issued a report on the T. Don Hutto facility and the Berks County Shelter Care Facility. These are the only two units in the country that house immigrant families. See Women's Commission for Refugee Women and Children (2007).

80. Patricia J. Ruland (2007).

81. Trent Lott (2007). Lott was actually a supporter of the 2007 Senate immigration bill that was defeated in June 2007.

82. Quoted in Michael Sandler (2007).

83. Mike Madden and Daniel Gonzalez (2007). Also see Robert G. Gonzales (2007). An example of the erroneous information spread by the Center for Immigration Studies can be found in the group's October 23, 2007 news release, "DREAM Act Offers Amnesty to 2.1 Million." This news release claimed that the DREAM Act would result in the legalization of parents and siblings, which was patently incorrect. See Center for Immigration Studies (2007).

84. Associated Press (2006); Mike Madden (2006).

85. Jonathan Weisman (2006); Suzanne Gamboa (2006).

86. *Tucson Citizen* (2006).

87. Nicole Gaouette (2007); Eric Lipton (2007).

88. Senator Edward Kennedy is quoted in the *New York Times* as saying, "It's a matter of our national security. We have broken borders and a broken immigration system." Commerce Secretary Carlos Gutierrez, another proponent, said, "This is a national security bill. We are fixing a national security problem." See Robert Pear (2007).

89. Preston (2007).

90. See Gaouette (2007).

91. Nancy Perkins (2007).

92. Lynh Bui and Beth Duckett (2007).

93. Jackie Alexander (2006). See chapter 4 for information on the C of CC.

94. See the Minuteman Civil Defense Corps' press release, "Simcox Addressed March for America," June 15, 2007, http://www.minute manhq.com/hq/article .php?sid=382 (accessed June 20, 2007). This press release reports that Simcox met with Representative Adam Putnam (R-FL) but was refused a meeting with Senator Mitch McConnell (R-KY).

95. Jeff Zeleny (2007). Other senators who received menacing messages include Mel Martinez (R-FL), Richard Burr (R-NC), and John Warner (R-VA). Graham reported that other senators had told him privately of threats.

96. Chris Barge (2007).

97. Romero (2007).

98. McCombs (April 30, 2007); Moreno (2007).

99. Frank Sharry, director of immigrant advocate group the National Immigration Forum, says that NumbersUSA has yet to make a dent at the ballot box. See Gaouette (2007).

100. Sandler (2007).

101. The poll was conducted on June 26, 2007 and is available at http://www.azpbs.org/horizon/poll/2007/6-26-07.htm. Pearce is quoted in Howard Fischer (2007).

102. Laurence Downs (2007).

103. See "New SPLC Report: Nation's most prominent anti-immigration group has history of hate, extremism" in the Southern Poverty Law Center's December 2007 Intelligence Report, http://www.scplcenter.org/news/item.jsp?aid= 295&printable=1.

104. Pew Hispanic Center (2007).

105. Kelly Davis (2007).

106. Melissa Ludwig (2007).

107. See http://www.leadershipinstitute.org.

108. Colby Sledge (2007).

109. Mike Glover (2007); Michael Cooper and Paul Vitello (2007).

# Bibliography

Please note that several Web sites referenced in this study are no longer available and some online documents, announcements, etc. have been removed. The author has copies of such referenced items.

Abraham, Yvonne. "Minuteman Project Founder Finds Inspiration in Concord." *Boston Globe*, December 14, 2006.

Abrahams, Ray. *Vigilant Citizens: Vigilantism and the State.* Cambridge, UK: Polity Press, 1998.

Adams, Suzanne. "Minutemen Call for City Ordinance." *Kingman Daily Miner*, November 16, 2006.

Agamben, Giorgio. *Homo Sacer: Sovereign Power and Bare Life.* Translated by Daniel Heller-Roazen. Stanford: Stanford University Press, 1998.

———. *Remnants of Auschwitz: The Witness and the Archive.* Translated by Daniel Heller-Roazen. New York: Zone Books, 2002.

———. *State of Exception.* Translated by Kevin Attell. Chicago: University of Chicago Press, 2005.

Agence France Presse. "U.S. Lawmakers Would Wall Mexico Border." *Immigrant Rights News.* November 4, 2005.

Alexander, Jackie. "Conservative Group Protests Illegal Aliens." *Daily Gamecock*, April 10, 2006.

Altamirano, Natasha. "Christian Groups Torn Over Illegals." *Washington Times*, January 14, 2007.

Albrecht, Leslie. "Immigration Sweep Nabs 51." *Merced Sun Star*, April 4, 2006.

Almeida, Christina. "Anti-Illegal Conference Opens." *Arizona Republic*, May 29, 2005, A4.

American Civil Liberties Union. "ACLU Challenges Prison-Like Conditions at Hutto Detention Center." American Civil Liberties Union. http://www.aclu .org/immigrants/detention/hutto.html.

———. "Anti-Immigrant Ordinances: Valley Park, MO." American Civil Liberties Union. http://www.aclu.org/im migrants/discrim/27858res20070105.html.

American Civil Liberties Union, American Friends Service Committee, and Witness. *Rights on the Line: Vigilantes at the Border.* Film. 2005. http://www .witness.org/index.php?option=com_rightsalert&Itemid=178&task=view& alert_id=43.

American Civil Liberties Union of New Jersey. *Behind Bars: The Failure of the Department of Homeland Security to Ensure Adequate Treatment of Immigrant Detainees in New Jersey.* American Civil Liberties Union, May 2007. http://www.aclu-nj.org/downloads/051507DetentionReport.pdf.

Andreas, Peter. *Border Games: Policing the U.S.-Mexico Divide.* Ithaca: Cornell University Press, 2000.

Anthony, Paul A. "Local KKK Group Planning to Rally." *San Angelo Standard Times,* August 8, 2006.

Anti-Defamation League. *Is FAIR Unfair?* Anti-Defamation League, 2000. http://www.adl.org/Civil_Rights/Is_Fair_Unfair.pdf.

———. *Border Disputes: Armed Vigilantes in Arizona.* Anti-Defamation League, 2003. http://www.adl.org/extremism/arizona/arizonaborder.pdf.

———. *White Revolution/Billy Roper.* Report. Anti-Defamation League, 2005. http://www.adl.org/learn/ext_us/w_revolution.asp?xpicked=3&item=wrbr.

———. "U.S. Anti-Immigrant Groups to Meet with Members of Racist European Party." Anti-Defamation League, 2007. http://www.adl.org/PresRele/DiRaB_41/4985_41.htm.

———. "Identity, Tradition and Sovereignty: A Who's Who." Anti-Defamation League, 2007. http://www.adl.org/main_Anti_SemitismInternational/identity_tradition_sovereignty.htm.

———. "The Ku Klux Klan Today." Anti-Defamation League, 2007. http://www.adl.org/learn/ext_us/kkk/intro.asp?learn.

———. "Jared Taylor/American Renaissance." Anti-Defamation League, 2008. http://www.adl.org./learn/ext_us/amren.asp?xpicked=5&item=amren.

Applebome, Peter. "Paramilitary Group That Caught 15 Aliens Plans More Patrols." *New York Times,* July 8, 1986, A15.

Archibold, Randal C. "A Border Watcher Finds Himself Under Scrutiny." *New York Times,* November 24, 2006.

———. "Arizona Governor Signs Tough Bill on Hiring Illegal Immigrants." *New York Times,* July 3, 2007.

*Arizona Republic.* "Sheriff's Posse to Patrol Desert." May 3, 2006.

———. "Deputies' ICE Training Results in Migrant Detentions." May 20, 2007.

Armond, Paul de. *Racist Origins of Border Militias: The History of White Supremacists Vigilantism and Tom Posey's Civilian Military Assistance.* Report. Public Good Project, 2005. http://www.publicgood.org/reports/vigilante_history.pdf.

Asaacson, Andy. "Minutemen Do the Dirty Work that 'Government' Won't Do." *San Francisco Chronicle,* May 8, 2005.

Ashcraft, Tom. "The Immigrant Invasion-Buchanan Declares 'State of Emergency Over Growing Threat." *Charlotte Observer,* September 2, 2006.

Associated Press. "New Mexico Minuteman Project Detects No Illegal Immigrants." *Arizona Daily Star,* October 3, 2005.

———. "Minuteman Group to Begin Building Border Fence on May 27." *Arizona Daily Star,* May 10, 2006.

———. "Immigrant Advocacy Groups Sue Over New Haven Raids." *Boston Globe,* August 11, 2007.

Bailey, Melissa. "DeStefano: Feds 'Terrorised' Fair Haven; Matos: This Won't Stop Us." *New Haven Independent,* June 6, 2007.

Baker, Peter. "Bush Set to Send Guard to Border." *Washington Post,* May 15, 2006, A01.

Banerjee, Neela. "New Coalition of Christians Seeks Changes at Borders." *New York Times,* May 8, 2007.

Barge, Chris. "Tancredo Wins Surprise Immigration Vote." *Rocky Mountain News,* June 15, 2007.

Barros, Lynda and Michele Waslin. "Immigrant Integration in Farmingville, NY and Dalton, GA: The Role of Community-Based Organizations." Prepared for *The Second Cumbre of the Great Plains' Re-Visioning Latino America: New Perspectives on Migration, Transnationalism, and Integration,* Omaha, Nebraska, April 22–24, 2005.

Barry, Ellen. "It's 'Get These People Out of Town.' " *Los Angeles Times,* August 16, 2006.

Barry, Tom. "Immigration Reform Caucus." Silver City, NM: International Relations Center Right Web Profiles, October 2004. http://www.rightweb.irc-on line.org/org/irc.php.

———. "Restrictionism Resurgent in Post-9/11 Politics: Protect America Now?" International Relations Center Americas Program, December 3, 2004. http://americas.irc-online.org/columns/amprog/2004/0412pan.html.

———. "Anti-Immigrant Backlash on the Home Front." *NACLA Report on the Americas* 38, no. 6 (2005). http://www.nacla.org/art—display.php?art-2555.

———. "Politics of Class and Corporations." International Relations Center Americas Program, August 9, 2005. http://americas.irc-online.org/am/224.

———. *Immigration Debate: Politics, Ideologies of Anti-Immigration Forces.* Special report. International Relations Center Americas Program, June 17, 2005. http://www.americaspolicy.org/reports/2005/050ideologies.html.

———. "Tom Tancredo—Leader of the Anti-Immigrant Populist Revolt." International Relations Center Right Web Analysis, December 30, 2005. http://rightweb.irc-online.org/rw/3005.html.

———. " 'Common Sense' Immigration Reform—What's FAIR Got do to With It?" International Relations Center Americas Program, January 19, 2006. http://rightweb.irc-online.org/rw/3053.html.

———. "Tom Tancredo: Christian Crusader, Cultural Nationalist, and Iran Freedom Fighter." International Relations Center Right Web Analysis, May 24, 2006. http://rightweb.irc-online.org/rw/3281.

Baum, Dan. "On the Border." *Los Angeles Times Magazine*, March 16, 2003.

Beal, Tom and Ignacio Ibarra. "Border Trek Delivered Simcox to His Cause." *Arizona Daily Star*, December 6, 2002.

Beirich, Heidi. "Immigration: Getting the Facts Straight." News item. Southern Poverty Law Center, May 9, 2007. http://www.splcenter.org./intel/news//item.jsp?aid=255&site_area=1&printable=1.

Bender, Steven W. "Sight, Sound, and Stereotype: The War on Terrorism and Its Consequences for Latinas/os." *Oregon Law Review* 18(2002): 1153–1178.

Bennett, David H. *The Party of Fear: The American Far Right from Nativism to the Militia Movement.* New York: Vintage Books, 1995.

Bennett, William Finn. "Internet a Key Tool for Immigration Issue Organizations." *North County Times*, June 12, 2005.

Benson, Matthew. "Governor OKs Toughest Migrant-Hire Law in U.S." *Arizona Republic*, July 3, 2007.

Berestein, Leslie. "Feds Override Laws, Give OK to Border Fence." *San Diego Union Tribune*, September 15, 2005.

Berkowitz, Bill. "The Lou Dobbs Fear Factor." *WorkingForChange*, June 1, 2006. http://www.scoop.co.nz/stories/print.html?path=HL0606/S00036.htm.

———. "Christian Conservatives Call for End of 14ᵗʰ Amendment Citizenship Birthright." Media Transparency, January 16, 2007. http://www.mediatransparency.org/storyprinterfriendly.php?storyID=172.

———. "Immigration Politics Draws Attention of David Horowitz." Media Transparency, August 19, 2005. http://www.mediatransparency.org/storyprinterfriendly.php?storyID=80.

Bernstein, Nina. "U.S. Raid on an Immigrant Household Deepens Anger and Mistrust." *New York Times*, April 10, 2007.

Berry, Jahna. "Smuggling Law Gets a Conviction." *Arizona Republic*, January 20, 2006.

———. "Human Smuggling Verdict Tossed." *Arizona Republic*, December 6, 2006.

Blumenthal, Max. "Republicanizing the Race Card." *The Nation*, March 23, 2006.

———. "A Look at the Forces Behind the Anti-Immigrant Movement." Amy Goodman interview on *Democracy Now*, May 2, 2007. http://www.democracynow.org/2007/5/2/a_look_at_the_forces_behind.

Blumenthal, Ralph. "Texas Lawmakers Put New Focus on Illegal Immigration." *New York Times*, November 16, 2006.

Bolton, Alexander. "GOP Preps for Talk Radio Confrontation." *The Hill*, June 27, 2007.

Bonner, T.J. Testimony before the Committee on Government Reform. United States House of Representatives, May 12, 2005. http://reform.house.gov/GovReform/Hearings/EventSingle.aspx?EvntID'26723.

Border Action Network. "Jury To AZ Border Vigilante: Guilty." Press release. November 22, 2006.

Bowers, Faye. "A New Arizona Law That Denies Bond to Suspected Illegal Immigrants Charged With Crime Faces Its First Legal Challenge Tuesday." *Christian Science Monitor*, May 22, 2007.

Braswell, Gentry. "Border Group to Conduct its First Operations Today in Palominas." *Sierra Vista Herald*, August 17, 2007.

Briscoe, Daren. "Return to Sender: While the Pols Debate Ways to Keep Illegal Immigrants Out, the Feds are Cracking Down on Those Already In-Country." *Newsweek*, July 24, 2006. http://kaskus.us/archive/index.php/t-356150.html.

Brooks, Karen. "Citizen Patrols Try to Shed Vigilante Image." *Dallas Morning News*, November 8, 2005.

Brown, Jim. "More Americans Killed by Illegal Aliens than Iraq War, Study Says." *Agape Press*, February 22, 2007.

Brown, Richard Maxwell. *Strain of Violence-Historical Studies of American Violence and Vigilantism*. New York: Oxford University Press, 1975.

—— "The History of Vigilantism in America." In *Vigilante Politics*. Edited by H. Jon Rosenbaum and Peter C. Sederberg, 79–109. Philadelphia: University of Pennsylvania Press, 1976.

Buchanan, Patrick J. *State of Emergency: The Third World Invasion and Conquest of America*. New York: Thomas Dunne Books St. Martin's Press, 2006.

Buchanan, Susy. "Nativism on the Air." *Southern Poverty Law Center Intelligence Report*, winter 2005. http://www.splc.org/itel.intelreport/article.jsp?aid=590&printable=1.

——. "Vigilante Justice." *Southern Poverty Law Center Intelligence Report*, spring 2007.

Buchanan, Susy and David Holthouse. "Playing Rough." *Southern Poverty Law Center Intelligence Report*, fall 2005.

——. "The Franchise." *Southern Poverty Law Center Intelligence Report*, fall 2005.

——. "Border Guardians Leader Calls for Violence." *Hispanic News*, April 24, 2006.

——. "Locked and Loaded." *The Nation*, August 28, 2006.

——. "Shoot, Shovel, Shut Up." *Southern Poverty Law Center Intelligence Report*, spring 2007. http://www.splcenter.org/intel.intelreport/article.jsp?aid=763.

Buchanan, Susy and Tom Kim. "The Nativists." *Southern Poverty Law Center Intelligence Report*, winter 2005. http://www.splcenter.org/intel/intelreport/article.jsp?aid=576&printable=1.

Bui, Lynh and Beth Duckett. "Hundreds Protest at Arizona Capitol for Tougher Immigration Laws." *Arizona Republic*, June 16, 2007.

Burghart, Devin. "Do It Yourself Border Cops." *Public Eye Magazine*, winter 2005. http://www.publiceye.org/magazine/v19n3burghart_cops.html.

——. "Black America Chose." Building Democracy Initiative of the Center for New Community, January 31, 2007. http://buildingdemocracy.org/index.php ?option=com_content&task=view&id=940&Itemid=10002.

Calderón, Sara Inés. "Minuteman Movement Inspiring Startups." *Brownsville Herald*, September 13, 2005.

Camarota, Steven and Mark Krikorian. "The Minutemen's Success." *Washington Times*, May 13, 2005.

Capps, Randy, Rosa Maria Castaneda, Ajay Chaudry and Robert Santos. *Paying the Price: The Impact of Immigration Raids on America's Children*. Report. Urban Institute for the National Council of La Raze, 2007. http://www.urban .org/uploadedPDF/41566.

Carroll, Susan. "Supremacists a Border Worry: FBI, Civilian Group are Concerned about Racists Joining Border Sweeps Next Month." *Tucson Citizen*, March 5, 2005.

Castillo, Victor. "Mexican Government Reacts to Minutemen's Presence on the Border." KGBT 4, Rio Grande Valley, Texas, March 28, 2007.

Center for Immigration Studies. "DREAM Act Offers Amnesty to 2.1 Million." Press release. October 23, 2007. http://www.cis.org/articles/2007/dreamact release.html.

Center for New Community. "The Coalition for the Future American Worker." Background brief. January 1, 2004.

——. "CNC Replies to FAIR Press Release." Building Democracy Initiative of the Center for New Community, August 10, 2004. http://www.buildingdemoc racy.org/index2.php?option=com_content&task=view&id=683.www.build ingdemocracy.org/reports/CFAW.pdf.

——. "White Nationalist Staffs US Immigration Reform PAC." Building Democracy Initiative of the Center for New Community, October 29, 2004. http:// buildingdemocracy.org/index.php?option=com_content&task=view&id= 13&Itemid=44.

——. *Federation for American Immigration Reform*. Center for New Community, November 2004. http://www.buildingdemocracy.org/reports/fair2004.pdf.

——. *Americans for Legal Immigration (ALI-PAC): Xenophobia, Nativism, and Anti-Immigrant Hysteria*. Center for New Community, June 2005. http:// www.buildingdemocracy.org/ali-pac.pdf.

——. *Shell Games: The "Minutemen" and Vigilante Anti-Immigrant Politics*. Center for New Community, October 2005. http://www.gcir.org/system/files/ shellgames.pdf.

——. "TN Talk Show Host Calls for Shooting of Immigrants." Building Democracy Initiative of the Center for New Community, April 28, 2006. http:// bdi.newcomm.org/index2.php?option=comm_content&task=view&id= 681Itemid=44.

——. "Raymondville: Inside the Largest Immigration Prison Camp in the United

States." *Democracy Now*, February 23, 2007. http://www.democracynow.org/article.pl?sid=07/02/23/1536249.

——. "Vlaams Belang in the USA." Building Democracy Initiative of the Center for New Community, April 1, 2007. http://buildingdemocracy.org/index.php?option=com_content&task=view&id=1075&Itemid=10002.

——. *American Immigration Control.* Center for New Community. http://www.buildingdemocracy.org/reports/American_Immigration_Control.pdf.

Center for Security Policy. Web site. http://www.centerforsecuritypolicy.org.

Cepeda, Esther J. "Talk Shows Pour Fire on Immigration Debate." *Chicago Sun Times*, August 7, 2007.

Christian Broadcasting Network. "Evangelical Leaders Get Involved in Immigration Debate." *The Brody File*, January 5, 2007. http://www.cbn.com/CBN news/82719.aspx?option=print.

Clark, Jonathan. "Second Civil Suit Against Barnett Moving Toward Trial." *Sierra Vista Herald*, September 12, 2006.

——. "ETMs File Complaint Against Barnett." *Sierra Vista Herald*, January 9, 2007.

Clark, Lesley. "Colorado Congressman Calls Miami a 'Third World Country.'" *Miami Herald*, November 27, 2006.

Coates, James. "Border Commandos Have U.S. on Edge." *Chicago Tribune*, July 13, 1986.

Cobb, Kim. "Oklahoma Immigration Bill Casts One of the Widest Nets." *Houston Chronicle*, April 23, 2007.

Collom, Lindsey. "54 Jailed Under 'Coyote' Statute." *Arizona Republic*, March 3, 2006, B1-B2.

——. "Sheriff Checking Migrant Status in Traffic Stops." *Arizona Republic*, March 30, 2007.

Congressional Immigration Reform Caucus. "Comment from CIRC Members on Minutemen." April 27, 2005. http://tancredo.house.gov/pressers/04.27.05 %20circ%20mm%20presser.htm.

——. "Naco Sector, Arizona U.S.-Mexico Border. A Field Report." May 19, 2005. http://www.house.gov/list/speech/ga09_norwrrod/MinutemanRepot.html.

Congressional Research Service. "Civilian Border Patrol Organizations: An Overview and History of the Phenomenon." Memo to the House Committee on the Judiciary. September 7, 2005.

——. *Border Security and the Southwest Border: Background, Legislation, and Issues.* September 28, 2005. http://www.au.af.mil/au/awc/awcgate/crs/rl33106.pdf.

Constable, Pamela. "'No Amnesty' Is Cry at D.C. Immigration Protest." *Washington Post*, April 23, 2007, B01.

Contreras, Franc. "Living by the US-Mexico Barrier." BBC News, February 27, 2006. http://news.bbc.co.uk/1/hi/world/americas/4743190.stm.

Coomes, Jessica. "Most in Poll Back Laws Aimed at Illegal Migrants." *Arizona Republic*, February 28, 2007.

———. "Experts: Border Issues Draw Hate Groups." *Arizona Republic*, March 14, 2007.

Cooper, Marc. "The 15-Second Men." *Los Angeles Times*, May 1, 2005.

———. "High Noon on the Border." *The Nation*, June 6, 2005.

Cooper, Michael and Paul Vitello. "Immigration Moves to Front and Center of G.O.P. Race." *New York Times*, December 12, 2007.

Cornelius, Wayne A. "Controlling 'Unwanted' Immigration: Lessons from the United States, 1993–2004." *Journal of Ethnic and Migration Studies* 31, no. 4 (2005): 775–794.

Cornelius, Wayne A., Takeyuki Tsuda, Philip L. Martin, and James F. Hollifield, eds. *Controlling Immigration: A Global Perspective.* 2nd edition. Stanford: Stanford University Press, 2004.

Council of Conservative Citizens. "A Statement of Principles of the Council of Conservative Citizens." http://www.cofcc.org/manifest.htm.

Cowan, Alison Leigh. "New Haven: Mayor Seeks Halt to Immigration Raids." *New York Times*, June 12, 2007.

Craig, Tim. "House Proposes Tough Laws; Senate Objects to Some." *Washington Post*, February 2, 2007.

Crawford, Amanda J. "Pearce Sorry for Sending White Separatist Article." *Arizona Republic*, October 10, 2006.

Crawford, James. "Anatomy of the English-Only Movement." Conference paper. University of Illinois at Urbana-Champaign, March 21, 1996. http://ourworld compuserve.com/homepages/JWCRAWFORD/anatomy.htm.

*Daily Texan.* "Construction Begins on Detention Center for Illegal Immigrants." June 22, 2006.

Dallacroce, Michelle. Post on Mothers Against Illegal Aliens Web site. December 6, 2007. http://www.mothersagainstillegalaliens.org.

Davidson, Miriam. "Vigilantes Hunt Down Immigrants." *Arizona Republic*, December 8, 2002.

Davis, Kelly. "Your Fellow Americans: Immigration Debates is a Breeding Ground for Ugly, Anonymous Commentary." *San Diego City Beat*, December 4, 2007. http://www.sdcitybeat.com/cms/story/detail/?id=6427.

Davis, Mike. "Pinkertons, Klansmen, and Vigilantes." In *No One Is Illegal: Fighting Racism and State Violence on the U.S.-Mexico Border.* Edited by Justin Akers Chacon and Mike Davis, 15–21. Chicago: Haymarket Books, 2006.

Deere, Stephen. "Archdiocese Helps Families Flee Valley Park Over Immigration Law." *St. Louis Today*, August 17, 2006.

De La Garza, Yvette, Greg Magnus, and Lisa Castro. "Crossing 'La Linea.'" *San Diego Union Tribune*, February 26, 2003.

Delson, Jennifer. "One Man's Convictions Launched a Border Crusade." *Los Angeles Times*, April 11, 2005.

Department of Homeland Security. *Treatment of Immigration Detainees Housed at Immigration and Customs Enforcement Facilities*. Department of Homeland Security, Office of Inspector General, OIG-07-01, December 2006. http://www.dhs.gov/xoig/assets/mgmtrpts/OIG_07-01_Dec06.pdf.

———. "The ICE T. Don Hutto Family Residential Facility: Maintaining Family Unity, Enforcing Immigration Laws." Fact sheet. Immigration and Customs Enforcement, January 2007. http://www.ice.gov/pi/news/factsheets/huttodetentionfac.htm.

Dorell, Oren and William M. Welch. "Local Police Confront Illegal Immigrants." *USA Today*, March 29, 2007.

Doty, Roxanne Lynn. "Desert Tracts: Statecraft in Remote Places." *Alternatives* 26 (2001): 523–543.

———. "The Double-Writing of Statecraft: Exploring State Responses to Illegal Immigration." *Alternatives* 21 (1996): 171–189.

———. "Immigration and the Politics of Security." *Security Studies* 8, no. 2 (1998–99): 71–93.

———. *Anti-Immigrantism in Western Democracies: Statecraft, Desire, and the Politics of Exclusion*. London and New York: Routledge RIPE Series in Global Political Economy, 2003.

Downs, Lawrence. "Showdown in Arizona, Where Mariachis and Minutemen Collide." *New York Times*, December 10, 2007.

Dunn, Timothy J. *The Militarization of the U.S.-Mexico Border 1978–1992*. Austin: University of Texas Center for Mexican American Studies, 1996.

Earl, John. "Immigration Reformer Wants to Send 20 Million Immigrants Back to Mexico and Start a Revolution There." *Orange County Observer*. July 14, 2005.

*Economist*. "The Tancredo Tendency." April 8, 2006, 36.

———. "Illegal but useful." November 3, 2007, 39.

Edelman, Murray. *Constructing the Political Spectacle*. Chicago: University of Chicago Press, 1988.

Enriquez, Susana. "Court Asked to Require Warrants for Immigration Raids." *Newsday*, October 8, 2007.

Esbenshade, Jill. *Divisions and Dislocation: Regulating Immigration through Local Housing Ordinances*. Immigration Policy Center, 2007. http://www.ailf.org/ipc/special_report/SpecialReport0907.pdf.

Eviatar, Daphne. "Nightly Nativism." *The Nation*, February 28, 2006.

FactCheck.org. "Even Opponents Call Iowa Anti-Immigration and Factually Accurate." January 12, 2004. http://www.factcheck.org/print_even_opponents_call_iowa_anit-immigration_ad_factually.html.

Fairness and Accuracy in Reporting. "Questions about Source in Immigration Debate." Press release. 1993. http://www.fair.org/index.php?page=2501.

——. "CNN's Immigration Problem: Is Dobbs the Exception Or the Rule?" April 24, 2006. http://www.fair.org/index.php?page=2867.

Fears, Darryl. "Illegal Immigrants Targeted by States." *Washington Post*, June 25, 2006, A01.

Federation for American Immigration Reform (FAIR). Newsletter. May 2007. http://www.fairus.org/site/PageServer?pagename=research_may07n102.5/5/07.

——. "Chicano Nationalism, Revanchism, and the Aztlan Myth." January 2005. http://www.fairus.org/site/PageServer?pagename=iic_immigrationissuecenters861a.

——. "Black Americans Organize to Fight for Immigration Reform." FAIR newsletter, July 2006. http://www.fairus.org/site/PageServer?pagename=research_jul06n104?.

——. Newsletter. June 2007. http://www.fairus.org.

——. Newsletter. May 2005. http://www.fairus.org.

Feldman, Megan. "The Hunted: Minutemen Train Their Sights on a New Target: Hispanic Day Laborers." *Dallas Observer*, December 14, 2006.

Fischer, Howard. "AZ Survey Would Legalize 12M." *Arizona Daily Star*, June 27, 2007.

Flynn, Michael. "Family Security Matters." International Relations Center Right Web Profiles, July 17, 2006. http://rightweb.irc-online.org/profile/3368.

Francis, Sam. "The Federal Government Has Met the Enemy and They Are the Tombstone Militia." VDare, December 30, 2002. http://www.vdare.com/francis/border.

Gamboa, Suzanne. "Groups Compare Texas, Pennsylvania Immigrant Facilities to Jails." *USA Today*, February 22, 2007.

Gamboa, Suzanne. "Bush Signs Mexico Fence Bill." *New York Times*, October 26, 2006.

Gaouette, Nicole. "Immigration Bill Ignites Grass-Roots Fire." *Los Angeles Times*, June 24, 2007.

——. "Border Issue Moves into Landowners' Yards." *Los Angeles Times*, December 8, 2007.

Gaouette, Nicole and Miguel Bustillo. "Immigration's Net Binds Children Too." *Los Angeles Times*, February 10, 2007.

Gaynor, Tim. "Feuding Minutemen Only United on Border Woes." Reuters, August 16, 2006. http://today.reuters.com/misc/PrinterFriendlyPopup.aspx?type=domesticNews&storyID=2.

Geyer, Georgie Anne. "Minutemen Project Backs Up An Overextended Border Patrol." *Yahoo! News*, April 26, 2005. http://news.yahoo.com/s/ucgg/minutemenprojectbacksupanoverextendedborderpatrol&print.

Gilchrist, Jim. Open letter. April 18, 2005. http://www.minutemanproject.com/info/letter_jg_2005apr18.html.

——. "Ex-Official at Agency Guilty of Harboring Illegal Resident." E-mail received by author. December 20, 2007.

——. "Gilchrist Bulletin." American Border Patrol Web site. http://www.americanpatrol.com/05-features/050719-mmp-needs-aid-campo/m.

Gilchrist, Jim and Jerome R. Corsi. *Minutemen: The Battle to Secure America's Borders*. Los Angeles: World Ahead Publishing, Inc., 2006.

Glazov, Jamie. "White Nationalism: A Symposium." *Front Page Magazine*, January 10, 2003. http://www.frontpagemag.com/Articles/Printable.asp?ID=5480.

Glover, Mike. "Huckabee Gets Minuteman Head's Backing." *Washington Post*, December 11, 2007.

Goldman, Adam. "Protests Hit Illegal Immigration Summit." *Washington Post*, May 29, 2005.

Gonzalez, Daniel. "States Fight Illegal Immigration." *Arizona Republic*, August 2, 2006.

——. "Web Site Targeting Employers of Migrants." *Arizona Republic*, January 11, 2007.

——. "Deputies May Start Arresting Migrants." *Arizona Republic*, January 13, 2007.

——."Officers Get Nod to Train to Enforce Immigration Laws." *Arizona Republic*, February 8, 2007.

——. "3 Students Deported to Mexico." *Arizona Republic*, March 15, 2007, B1 & B5.

——. "Migrant-bill Backlash Targets Talk Radio." *Arizona Republic* July 10, 2007.

Gonzalez, Daniel, Dennis Wagner, and Susan Carroll. "Armed Border Groups Still a Risk." *Arizona Republic*, September 18, 2004, B1.

Gonzales, Robert G. "Wasted Talent and Broken Dreams: The Lost Potential of Undocumented Students." Immigration Policy Center, October 19, 2007. http://www.ailf.org/ipc/infocus/WastedTalent.pdf.

Gorania, Jay. "Several Protesters Arrested at Ku Klux Klan Rally." *Odessa American*, June 18, 2006. http://www.oaoa.com/news/nw061806e.htm.

Gregory, Alan. "Ku Klux Klan Group Supports Barletta." *Standard-Speaker*, March 21, 2007. http://www.standardspeaker.com/index2.php?option=com_content&task=view&id=4737&.

Gregory, Dick. *NBC Evening News*. KPNX Channel 12, Phoenix, Arizona, June 14, 2007.

Griswold, Daniel T. "Congressman Uses Sept. 11 Terrorism to Advance Anti-Immigration Agenda." Cato Institute, November 18, 2001. http://www.cato.org/dailys/11-18-01.html.

Hall, Randy. "Illegal Aliens Waging 'Silent War' on the US, Says Minuteman Activist." *Cybercast News Service*, January 19, 2007.

Hannity, Sean, and Alan Colmes. *Hannity & Colmes.* Television show. Fox Broadcasting Company, April 8, 2005. Accessed through LexisNexis.

———. *Hannity & Colmes.* Television show. Fox Broadcasting Company, August 30, 2006, transcript 083001cb253.

———. *Hannity & Colmes.* Television show. Fox Broadcasting Company, April 18, 2006. Accessed through LexisNexis.

———. *Hannity & Colmes.* Television show. Fox Broadcasting Company, April 19, 2006. Accessed through LexisNexis.

———. *Hannity & Colmes.* Television show. Fox Broadcasting Company, April 26, 2006. Accessed through LexisNexis.

Hansen, Thomas Blom, and Finn Stepputat. *Introduction to Sovereign Bodies: Citizens, Migrants, and States in the Postcolonial World.* Princeton: Princeton University Press, 2005.

Harris, Shane. "Immigration Enforcement Raid Sparks Outcry." Daily briefing. GovExec.com, April 13, 2007. http://www.govexec.com/story_page.cfm?articleid=36615&printerfriendlyVers=1&.

Hawley, Chris. "Mexico Decries Civilian Border Patrol." *Arizona Republic,* March 2, 2005.

Hayes, Christopher. "Keeping America Empty." *In These Times,* April 24, 2007.

Hendricks, Tyche. "Militias Round Up Illegal Aliens in Desert." *San Francisco Chronicle,* May 31, 2004.

Hermann, William. "Boost in Migrant Arrests Spurs Housing Need." *Arizona Republic,* June 15, 2007.

Hess, Bill. "Vigilante or Minuteman? Rancher Goes High-Tech to Nab Immigrants, Smugglers." *Sierra Vista Herald,* July 27, 2002.

Hogan, Shanna. "Protesters State Views, Trade Insults Near Mexican Consulate." *East Valley Tribune,* April 23, 2006, A8.

Hollifield, James F. "The Politics of International Migration—How Can We Bring the State Back In?" In *Migration Theory: Talking Across Disciplines.* Edited by Caroline B. Brettell and James F. Hollifield. New York and London: Routledge, 2000.

Holstege, Sean. "States Tackle Migrant Issue." *Arizona Republic,* June 26, 2007.

Hsu, Spencer S. "Immigrants Mistreated, Report Says." *Washington Post,* January 17, 2007.

Hsu, Spencer S. and Krissah Williams. "Illegal Workers Arrested in 6-State ID Theft Sweep." *Washington Post,* December 13, 2006.

Hsu, Spencer S., and Sylvia Moreno. "Border Policy's Success Strains Resources." *Washington Post,* February 2, 2007.

Hurt, Charles. "Immigration Debate Gets Religious." *Washington Times,* January 8, 2007.

Huslin, Anita. "On Immigration, A Theorist Who's No Fence-Sitter." *Washington Post*, November 26, 2006, D01.

Huysmans, Jef. "Minding Exception: The Politics of Insecurity and Liberal Democracy." *Contemporary Political Theory* 3 (2004): 321–341.

Ibarra, Ignacio. "Tombstone Paper Calls for Militia." *Arizona Daily Star*, November 15, 2002.

International Relations Center. "Social Contract Press." Somerville, NM: Interhemispheric Resource Center, August 2004. http://rightweb.irc-online.org/profile/1539.html.

Jacobs, Andrew. "An Immigrant Segment by Radio's 'Jersey Guys' Draws Fire." *New York Times*, March 23, 2007.

Jacobson, David. *Rights Across Borders: Immigration and the Decline of Citizenship*. Baltimore: Johns Hopkins University Press, 1997.

Jarvie, Jenny. "Lawsuit Says Latino Citizens Were Caught Up In Raids Seeking Illegal Immigrants." *Los Angeles Times*, November 2, 2006.

Johnson, Jeff. "Citizens Patrol Southern U.S. Border to Stop Illegal Aliens." *The Nation*, December 13, 2002.

Johnson, Kevin. "Feds Watching Anti-Immigrant Extremists." *USA Today*, May 20, 2007.

Jonas, Susanne. "Reflections on the Great Immigration Battle of 2006 and the Future of the Americas." *Social Justice* 33, no. 1(2006): 6–19.

Jordan, Lara Jakes. "Minutemen to Patrol Arizona Border." *Washington Post*, February 21, 2005.

Keilman, John. "Hispanics Rue City's New Rules." *Chicago Tribune*, October 29, 2006.

Kelley, Josh. "Migrants in Adult Ed Facing Expulsion Soon." *Arizona Republic*, January 26, 2007.

Ketcham, Christopher. "The Angry Patriot." Salon.com, May 11, 2005. http://salon.com/story/news/feature/2005/05/11/minuteman.

Keyes, Alan. Keynote speech at the Minuteman Civil Defense Corps's fence groundbreaking in May 2006. Transcript. RenewAmerica, June 7, 2006. http://www.renewamerica.us/news/060607keyes.htm.

——. Speech made for Minuteman Civil Defense Corps in October 2006. Transcript and audio clip. Minuteman Civil Defense Corps, October 2006. http://www.Minutemanhq.com/video/keyes_transcript.php.

Kiefer, Michael. "Migrants Challenge Smuggling Charges." *Arizona Republic*, May 4, 2006.

——. "Migrant Crime Numbers Proportionate to Population." *Arizona Republic*, May 8, 2007.

Kil, Sang, and Cecilia Menjivar. "The 'War on the Border': Criminalizing Immigrants and Militarizing the U.S.-Mexico Border." In *Immigration and Crime:*

*Race, Ethnicity and Violence*. Edited by Ramiro Martinez Jr. and Abel Valenzuela. New York: New York University Press, 2006.

Knickerbocker, Brad. "Anti-Immigration Fuels KKK Resurgence." *Christian Science Monitor*, February 10, 2007.

Kouri, Jim. "43 Conservative Leaders Pledge to Withhold Support for Lawmakers Voting for Amnesty." *American Chronicle*, July 6, 2006. http://www.americanchronicle.com/articles/viewArticle.asp?articleID=11295.

Krikorian, Mark. "Keeping Terror Out: Immigration and Asymmetric Warfare." *The National Interest*, no. 75 (spring 2004). http://www.cis.org/articles/2004/mskoped050104.html.

——. "Strange Bedfellows." *National Review Online*. http://www.national review.com/comment/krikorian20040331036.asp.

——. "A Third Way." *Palm Beach Post*, May 7, 2006.

Kundani, Arum Kundani. "How the BNP Entered the Political Mainstream." *Independent Race and Refugee News Network*, May 4, 2006. http://www.irr.org.uk/2006/may/ak000011.html.

Lares, Carlos. "2005 Georgia Christian Coalition Conference—Immigration Reform Panel." March 23, 2005. http://www.galeo.org/pdfs/2005GACristian Coaltion.pdf.

Larralde, Carlos M., and Richard Griswold del Castillo. "San Diego's Ku Klux Klan." *Journal of San Diego History 1920–1980* 46, no. 2–3 (spring/summer 2000).

League of the South. "Southern Unity." March 2005. http://dixient.org/dn-gazette/southern-unity.htm.

Leatherman, Jackie. "Minutemen Picket Day Labor Hiring." *East Valley Tribune*, December 4, 2006.

Lelyveld, Joseph. "The Border Dividing Arizona." *New York Times Sunday Magazine*, October 15, 2006. http://www.ntimes.com/2006/10/15/magazine/15im migration.html?ei=5094&en=d643b.

Lemons, Stephen. "Burn, Baby, Burn." *Phoenix New Times*, February 15, 2007, 14–33.

Levine, Jeremy and Landon Van Soest. *Walking the Line*. Film. 2005. http://www.walkingthelinemovie.com.

Lichtblau, Eric. "Prosecutions in Immigration Doubled in Last Four Years." *New York Times*, September 29, 2005.

Lipton, Eric. "Give Officials Access, Landowners on Border Are Told." *New York Times*, December 8, 2007.

Llorente, Elizabeth. "Radio Station's Campaign Shocks Latino Community." *Arizona Republic*, March 22, 2007.

Loew, Morgan. "5 Investigates Follows Up on Lawless and Border Guardians." CBS News 5, Phoenix, Arizona, April 9, 2006. http://www.kpho.com/iteam/9528678/detail.html.

LoMonaco, Claudine. "Saturday Rally Kicks Off Minuteman Border Watch." *Tucson Citizen*, September 28, 2006.

——. "Immigration Attorneys Advising Clients to Avoid Driving." *Tucson Citizen*, March 27, 2007.

Londono, Ernesto. "Database is Tool in Deporting Fugitives." *Washington Post*, June 13, 2007.

Lott, Trent. Quote in "Verbatim" section. *Time Magazine*, July 9, 2007.

Ludden, Jennifer. "Supremacist Groups Use Immigration Issue to Recruit Members." *Morning Edition* radio program segment. National Public Radio, March 6, 2007. http://nl.newsbank.com/nl-search/we/Archives?p_action =doc&_docid=117B745D-35D0.

Ludwig, Melissa. "Response to Minuteman Boss Less Harsh." *San Antonio Express*, October 29, 2007.

Luo, Michael and Laurie Goodstein. "Emphasis Shift for New Breed of Evangelicals." *New York Times*, May 21, 2007.

Lydersen, Kari. "Church is Sanctuary As Deportation Nears." *Washington Post*, August 17, 2006, A10.

Madden, Mike. "President Pushes Guard Plan." *Arizona Daily Star*, May 16, 2006.

Madden, Mike and Daniel Gonzalez. "Senate Denies Legal Status of Children of Immigrants." *Arizona Republic*, October 25, 2007.

Maish, James H. "Anti-Alien Group Quits Campsite." *Arizona Daily Star*, July 7, 1986.

Mansfield, Duncan. "Migrant Patrols Take Root Nationally." *Arizona Daily Star*, July 18, 2005.

Margetts, Helen, Peter John, David Rowland, and Stuart Weir. "The BNP: The Roots of Its Appeal." Democratic Audit, Human Rights Centre. Colchester: University of Essex, 2006.

Marino, David. "Illegal Immigration Activist May Sue Over E-Mail from Mexican Flag Burner." KVOA News 4, Tucson, Arizona, May 14, 2006. http://kvoa.com/global/story.asp?s=4899698&ClientType=Printable.

Marino, Jonathan. "Border Agency Weighs Options to Handle Surge of Detainees." GovExec.com, June 5, 2006. http://www.gov.exec.com/dailyfed/0606/060506jl.htm.

——. "Report Alleges Mistreatment at Immigrant Detention Centers." GovExec .com, January 19, 2007. http://www.govexec.com/story_page.cfm?articleid= 35915&printerfriendlyVers=1&.

Marizco, Michael. "Border-Watch Group: All Talk?" *Arizona Daily Star*, February 22, 2005.

——. "Migrants Shift Entry to Dangerous West." *Arizona Daily Star*, April 19, 2005.

Martin, David. "Twilight Statuses: A Closer Examination of the Unauthorized Population." Policy brief. Migration Policy Institute, June 2005.

Massa, Justin and Cecilia Abundis. "The New Battleground." Building Democracy Initiative of the Center for New Community, February 1, 2007. http://www.buildingdemocracy.org/index2.php?opotion=com_content&task=view&id=957&.

Mattera, Philip, Mafruza Khan, and Stephen Nathan. *Corrections Corporation of America: A Critical Look at Its First Twenty Years.* Grassroots Leadership, the Corporate Research Project of Good Jobs First, and Prison Privatisation Report International, December 2003. http://www.goodjobsfirst.org/pdf/CCA%20Anniversary%20Report.pdf.

McCombs, Brady. "Group Says Entrants Adversely Affect Kids." *Arizona Daily Star*, February 19, 2006.

——. "New Congress Provides Impetus—Groups Jockey in a Daily Derby for Attention, Money, Credibility." *Arizona Daily Star*, January 28, 2007.

——. "Deaths Drop in Border Sector." *Arizona Daily Star*, September 29, 2006.

——. "Towers Scan Border. Arivaca is Upset Over Appearance, Lack of Privacy." *Arizona Daily Star*, April 30, 2007.

McConnell, Scott. "From Minutemen to Mainstream." *American Conservative*, September 26, 2005.

McDonnell, Patrick J. "Brash Evangelist." *Los Angeles Times Magazine*, June 15, 2001.

McGirk Douglas, Tim. "Border Clash." *Time Magazine*, June 26, 2000. http://www.time.com/time/magazine/article/0,9171,997279,00.html.

Media Matters. "Minuteman Organizer James Gilchrist Defends White Supremacists From Alan Colmes: 'Why Are You Picking On Them?'" April 6, 2005. http://www.medimatters.org/items/printable/200504060003.

——. "*Christian Science Monitor* Failed to Note Minuteman Project Volunteer's White Supremacist Ties." May 4, 2005. http://mediamatters.org/items/printable/200505040001.

——. "Savage: 'Burn the Mexican Flag!'" March 31, 2006. http://mediamatters.org/items/printable/20060331008.

——. "Buchanan Book Featured on *Today*: For Nation to 'Survive[],' U.S. Must Keep 'Americans of European Descent' From Becoming 'Minority.'" August 23, 2006. http://mediamatters.org/items/printable/200608230002.

——. "In Latest NBC Plug For Buchanan''s Anti-Immigrant Book, Matthews Declared That 'Thanks to This Show,' Book Will 'Probably' Remain 'Number One on Amazon.'" August 25, 2006. http://mediamatters.org/items/printable/200608250008.

——. "Hosting Segment From Hazelton, Pa., Dobbs Did Not Acknowledge Fundraising for the Embattled Town." May 9, 2007. http://media matters.org/items/printable/200705090007.

Media Transparency. *Center for Security Policy, Inc.* EIN: 52-1601976. 2006. http://www.mediatransparency.org/recipientgrantsprint.php?recipientID=489.

Medina, Jennifer. "Arrests of 31 in U.S. Sweep Bring Fear in New Haven." *New York Times*, June 8, 2007.

Meeks, Brock N. "Common Thread Binds Border Volunteers." MSNBC, June 10, 2005. http://www.msnbc.msn.com/id/7409293/print/1/displaymode/1098.

Merrill, Bruce, and Arizona's KAET-TV/Channel 8. Poll. http://www.azpbs.org/horizon/poll/2005/4-26-05htm.

Miller, Tom. *On The Border: Portraits of America's Southwestern Frontier*. Tucson, Arizona: University of Arizona Press, 1992.

Milliken, Mary. "Immigrant Labor Dilemma Hits California Beach Town." Reuters, July 17, 2006.

Minuteman Civil Defense Corps. "New MCDC Team Leads June Arizona Muster—MCDC SRT Save 6 Illegals from Death in Desert." http://www.minutemanhq.com/hq/borderops_25.php.

——. "Simcox Addressed March for America." Press release. June 15, 2007. http://www.minutemanhq.com/hq/article.php?sid=382.

Mock, Brentin. "Smokescreen." *Southern Poverty Law Center Intelligence Report*, fall 2006, 19–24.

Montini, E.J. "A Solution to Our Problems That Borders on Genius." *Arizona Republic*, May 1, 2005.

Moreno, Sylvia. "For Residents of Arizona Border Town, Towers Are Unwelcome Eyes in the Sky." *Washington Post*, June 10, 2007.

Moscoso, Eunice. "Radio Hosts Gather in D.C. to Blast Illegal Immigration." *Denver Post*, April 25, 2007.

Moser, Bob. "Rough Ride: Anti-Immigration Activists Confront a Pro-Migrant Freedom Ride." *Southern Poverty Law Center Intelligence Report*, winter 2003.

——. "Open Season: As Extremists Peddle Their Anti-Immigrant Rhetoric Along the Troubled Arizona Border, A Storm Gathers." *Southern Poverty Law Center Intelligence Report*, fall 2003.

Mouffe, Chantal, ed. *The Challenge of Carl Schmitt*. London and New York: Verso, 1999.

Mulkern, Anne C. "Firebrand Tancredo Puts Policy Over Party Line." *Denver Post*, September 4, 2006.

Mulloy, D.J. *American Extremism: History, Politics and the Militia Movement*. New York and London: Routledge, 2004.

Murray, Shailagh and T.R. Reid. "Tuning In to Anger on Immigration." *Washington Post*, March 31, 2006, A01.

Nagel, C.R. "Geopolitics by Another Name: Immigration and the Politics of Assimilation." *Political Geography* 21 (2002): 971–987.

Nakamura, Karen. "Republican's Rick Oltman Is Disturbing News." *Coastal Post*, June 1996. http://www.coastalpost.com/96/6/1.htm.

Nanez, Dianna M. " 'Don't Ask, Don't Tell' Immigration Era Ending." *Arizona Republic*, April 24, 2007.

National Association of Evangelicals. "Resolution on Immigration." October 12, 2006. http://www.nae.net/images/Resolution%20on%20 Immigration%20 -%20 October%202006.pdf.

National Conference of State Legislatures. "Overview of State Legislation Related to Immigration and Immigrants in 2007." http://www.ncsl.org/programs/ immig/2007StateLegislationImmigration.html.

——. "The History of Federal Requirements for State Issued Driver's Licenses and Identification Cards." http://www.ncsl.org/standcomm/sctran/His tory _of_DL_Reform.htm.

National Vanguard. "Tancredo Reacts to Illegal Immigration Rallies." April 12, 2006. http://www.nationalvanguard/org/printer.php?id=8620.

Nevins, Joseph. *Operation Gatekeeper: The Rise of the "Illegal Alien" and the Making of the U.S.-Mexico Boundary.* New York and London: Routledge, 2002.

*Newsday.* Untitled. August 11, 2007. http://www.newsday.com/news/local/wire/ connecticut/ny-bc-ct--immigrants-raid0811aug11,0,5.

*NewsHour.* "Tightening Borders." Public Broadcasting Service, January 1, 2002.

Norwood, Charlie. Untitled. *Tombstone Tumbleweed,* April 14, 2005.

Nyers, Peter. "No One Is Illegal Between City and Nation." Paper. Presented at the International Studies Association Conference, San Diego, California, March 22–25, 2006.

O'Connell, Stacey. Resignation letter. Minuteman Civil Defense Corps, December 1, 2006. http://forum.minutemanhq.comphpBB2/viewtopic.php?t=4840.

——. "In Closing: A Letter from Stacey O'Connell." Letter. Minuteman Civil Defense Corps, October 30, 2007. http://www.minutemanhq.com/state/read .php?chapter=AZ&sid=292.

O'Connor, Anahad. "In Brewster, a Backlash Against Day Laborers." *New York Times,* February 5, 2006.

Owens, Mackubin Thomas. "If the Gov't Won't Do It. . ." *National Review.* 2002. http://www.nationalreview.com/owens/owens112502.asp.

Passel, Jeffery S. *Estimates of the Size and Characteristics of the Undocumented Population.* Pew Hispanic Center, March 21, 2005. http://www.ime.gob.mx/ investigaciones/pew/2006/pew_migrant_population.pdf.

Pate, Hillary. "Minutemen, or Men of the Minute?" Heritage Foundation, April 26, 2005. http://www.heritage.org/Press/Commentary/ed042705a.cfm? RenderforPrint'1.

Pear, Robert. "Security is Focus of Revised Effort on Immigration." *New York Times,* June 14, 2007.

Pecoud, Antoine and Paul de Guchteneire. "International Migration, Border Controls and Human Rights: Assessing the Relevance of a Right to Mobility." *Journal of Borderland Studies* 21, no. 1 (spring 2006): 69–86.

Pela, Robert L. "One Nation Under Simcox." *Phoenix New Times*, April 14, 2005.

People for the American Way. "Religious Right Groups Join Immigration Debate." Right Wing Watch, January 9, 2007. http://www.rightwingratch.org/2007/01/religious_right_11.html.

——. "Immigration Debate Takes Dangerous Turn." July 14, 2006. http://www.pfaw.org/pfaw/general/default.aspx?oid=21758.

Perkins, Nancy. "Rally Targets Illegals." *Deseret Morning News*, June 7, 2007. http://deseretnews.com/dn/print/1,1442,660227409,00.htm.

Pew Hispanic Center. "The Immigration Debate: Controversy Heats Up, Hispanics Feel a Chill." December 13, 2007. http://pewresearch.org/pubs/659/immigration-debate.

Phelan, Daniel Kurtz. "Hands Up." *New Yorker*, December 12, 2005.

Pickel, Mary Lou. "30 Arrested in Immigration Raid Near Fort Benning." *Atlantic Journal Constitution*, November 1, 2007.

Pitzl, Mary Jo. "Legislative Interest in Immigration Explodes." *Arizona Republic*, December 2, 2007.

Pomfret, John and Sonya Geis. "One Sheriff Sees Immigration Answer as Simple." *Washington Post*, May 20, 2006, A03.

Porteus, Liza. "Feds Raid 6 Swift and Company Meatpacking Plants in Apparent Illegal Immigration Search." FOXNews.com, December 12, 2006. http://www.foxnews.com/printer_friendly_story/0,3566,236044.html.

*Portsmouth Herald*. "White Pride Rallies in N.H." http://archive.seacoastonline.com/news/07172006/nhnews-ph-nh-anti-immigration.html.

Powell, Michael and Michelle Garcia. "Pa. City Puts Illegal Immigrants on Notice." *Washington Post*, August 22, 2006, A03.

Preston, Julia. "U.S. Raids 6 Meat Plants in ID Case." *New York Times*, December 13, 2006.

——. "Grass Roots Roared and Immigration Plan Collapsed." *New York Times*, June 10, 2007.

——. "Immigration Quandry: A Mother Torn from Her Baby," *New York Times*, November 17, 2007.

*Publishers Weekly*. Book sale figures. Week of October 2, 2006. http://www.publishers weekly.com/index.asp?layout=bestsellerprint&imarketid=1&listdat.

Purcell, Mark and Joseph Nevins. "Pushing the Boundary: State Restructuring, State Theory, and the Case of U.S.-Mexico Border Enforcement in the 1990s." *Political Geography* 24 (2005): 211–235.

Reimers, David M. *Unwelcome Strangers: American Identity and the Turn Against Immigration*. New York: Columbia University Press, 1998.

Riccardi, Nicholas. "Anti-Illegal Immigration Forces Share a Wide Tent." *Los Angeles Times*, May 4, 2006.

Roberts, Laurie. "Maybe They're Nuts But Minutemen Have Been Effective." *Arizona Republic*, April 2, 2005, B10.

Roddy, Dennis. "Jared Taylor, A Racist in the Guise of 'Expert.'" *Pittsburgh Post Gazette*, January 23, 2005.

Romero, Anthony D. "We Are the Stories We Tell." *Civil Liberties: The American Civil Liberties Union National Newsletter*, summer 2007.

Ross, Melissa Nalani. "Profiles: Choose Black America Leadership." Building Democracy Project of the Center for New Community, January 31, 2007. http://buildingdemocracy.org/index.php?option=com_content&task=view&id=941&Itemid=10002.

Rotstein, Arthur. "Minuteman Group Begins Building its Border Fence." *Arizona Daily Star*, May 28, 2006.

Rozemberg, Hernan. "Concern That Borders on Fear." *San Antonio Express*, September 28, 2005.

Rubinkam, Michael. "Town's Immigration Law in Judge's Hands." *Washington Post*, March 24, 2007.

Ruland, Patricia J. "T. Don Hutto: Homeland Security Bars U.N. Inspector." *Austin Chronicle*, May 11, 2007.

Rumbaut, Ruben G., Roberto G. Gonzales, Golnas Komaie, and Charlie V. Morgan. "Debunking the Myth of Immigrant Criminality: Imprisonment Among First-and Second-Generation Young Men." Migration Policy Institute, *Migration Information Source*, June 1, 2007. http://www.migrationinformation.org/Feature/display.cfm?id=403.

Sanchez, Mary. "Racists Riding Wave of Anti-Immigrant Fervor." *Kansas City Star*, May 9, 2006.

Sandler, Michael. "Immigration: From the Capitol to the Courts." *Congressional Quarterly Weekly*, December 10, 2007.

Sarkar, Saurav. "Sidebar: Birth of a Factoid." Sidebar to "The False Debate over 'Broken Borders.'" Fairness and Accuracy in Reporting. April 20, 2007. http://www.fair.org/index.php?page=2899.

Saskia Sassen. "Regulating Immigration in a Global Age: A New Policy Landscape." *Parallax* 11, No. 1 (2005): 35–45.

Scarpinato, Daniel. "Denial of Bail to Entrants Pushed." *Arizona Daily Star*, June 10, 2007.

———. "Governor OKs Tough Employer Sanctions." *Arizona Daily Star*, July 3, 2007.

Schey, Peter A. "Vigilantism On U.S.-Mexico Border: An Analysis of Legal, Political, and Diplomatic Options." Center for Human Rights and Constitutional Law Foundation, March 2005. http://centerforhumanrights.org.

Schmitt, Carl. *The Concept of the Political*. Translated by George Schwab. Chicago: University of Chicago Press, 1996.

———. *Theology: Four Chapters on the Concept of Sovereignty*. Translated by George Schwab. Chicago: University of Chicago Press, 2005.

Schwartz, David and Tim Gaynor. "Citizens Group Set to Patrol U.S.-Mexico Border." Reuters, January 18, 2005.

Searing, Nate. "Ranch Rescue Disbands Douglas Operation Amid Internal Strife." *Sierra Vista Herald*, April 15, 2004.

Seper, Jerry. "Border Patrols Inspire Imitation." *Washington Times*, April 16, 2005.

——. "Minutemen Join New Organization." *Washington Times*, April 20, 2005.

——. "Minutemen Announce April Border Campaign." *Washington Times*, February 17, 2006.

——. "Ex-Minuteman Members Form Group." *Washington Times*, September 29, 2007.

Sheehy, Daniel. *Fighting Immigration Anarchy: American Patriots Battle to Save the Nation*. Bloomington, Indiana: Author House, 2005.

Simcox, Chris. "Enough is Enough." *Tombstone Tumbleweed*, October 24, 2002.

——. Editorial. *Tombstone Tumbleweed*, October 31, 2002.

——. Testimony before the Committee on Government Reform, United States House of Representatives. May 12, 2005.

——. Open letter. April 18, 2005. http://www.minutemanproject.com/info/let ter_cs_2005apir18.html.

Sledge, Colby. "Minuteman Leader Comes to Campuses." *Tennessean*, November 5, 2007.

Smith-Spark, Laura. " 'Vigilantes' Set for Mexico Border Patrol." BBC News, March 28, 2005. http://news.bbc.co.uk/2/hi/americas/4384855.stm.

SourceWatch. "Choose Black America." November 2006. http://www.source watch.org/index.php?title+Choose_Black_America.

Southern Poverty Law Center. *Southern Poverty Law Center Intelligence Report*, fall 2001.

——. "The Puppeteer." *Southern Poverty Law Center Intelligence Report*, summer 2002. http://www.splcenter.org/intelligenceproject/ip-4vl.html.

——. "SPLC Sues Immigration Agency." November 1, 2002. http://www.splcen ter.org/legal/news/article.jsp?aid=221&site_area=1&printable=1.

——. "White Supremacy—Ignoring Its Own Ties, Anti-Immigration Group Denounces White 'Separatist.' " *Southern Poverty Law Center Intelligence Report*, fall 2004. http://www.splcenter.org/intelreport/artile.jsp?aid=498.

——. "The Nativists." *Southern Poverty Law Center Intelligence Report*, winter 2005. http://www.splcenter.org/intel/intelreport/article.jsp?aid=576&print able=1.

——. "Extremist Leads New Arkansas Anti-Immigration Group." *Southern Poverty Law Center Intelligence Report*, January 5, 2005. http://www.splcenter.org/intel/news/item.jsp?aid=8.

——. "Immigrants Win Arizona Ranch." August 19, 2005. http://www.splcenter.org/legal/news/article.jsp?site_area=1&aid=125.

——. "Anti-Immigration Movement Using Hate Group Materials, Dobbs Slams Illegal Immigration." *Southern Poverty Law Center Intelligence Report*, summer 2006. http://www.splcenter.org/intelrepot/article.jsp?aid=639.

——. "New SPLC Report: Nation's Most Prominent Anti-Immigration Group Has History of Hate, Extremism." *Southern Poverty Law Center Intelligence Report*, December 11, 2007. http://www.splcenter.org/news/item.jsp?aid=295&printable=1.

Spencer, Mark. "New Haven's Immigration Drama Grows." *Courant*, June 15, 2005.

Sprengelmeyer, M.E. "Clergy Decry Tancredo Appearance." *Rocky Mountain News*, September 15, 2006.

Steller, Tim. "Armed Citizens Capture Pot Load." *Arizona Daily Star*, October 17, 2002.

Strohm, Chris. "Lawmakers Consider Using Military to Seal U.S. Borders." Gov Exec.com, April 28, 2005. http://www.govexec.com/story_page.cfm?articleid=31112.

Strum, Charles. "Follow-Up on the News: The Hanigan Case." *New York Times*, March 7, 1982.

Stull, Donald, Michael Broadway, and David Griffith, eds. *Any Way You Cut It: Meatpacking and Small-Town America*. Lawrence: University of Kansas Press, 1995.

Susman, Sahra. "Minuteman Group Calls Off Rally." *Daily Bulletin*, March 31, 2007. http://www.dailybulletin.com/prtlett/article/html/fragments/print_article.jsp?articleId=5568.

Swain, Carol M. *The New White Nationalism in America*. Cambridge, UK: Cambridge University Press, 2002.

Swarns, Rachel L. "Capitol's Pariah on Immigration is Now Power." *New York Times*, December 24, 2005.

Tancredo, Tom. Foreword to *Minutemen: The Battle to Secure America's Borders*. Los Angeles: World Ahead Publishing, 2006.

Tanton, John. "Memo to WITAN IV Attendees from John Tanton." October 10, 1986. *Southern Poverty Law Center Intelligence Report*, summer 2002. http://www.splcenter.org/intel/intelreport/article.jsp?sid=125&printable=1.

Taylor, Jared. "Africa in our Midst: Lessons from Katrina." American Renaissance, October 2005. http://www.amren.com/mtnews/archives/2005/09/africa_in_our_m.php.

Tedford, Deborah. "Armed U.S. Citizens Patrol Border with Mexico." Reuters, February 12, 2003.

Texeira, Erin. "New Report Says Hate Groups More Active." *Washington Post*, February 5, 2007.

Theiler, Tobias. "Societal Security and Social Psychology." *Review of International Studies* 29 (2003): 249–268.

*Time Magazine.*"10 Questions for Pat Buchanan." August 28, 2006, 6.

Transactional Records Access Clearinghouse. *TRAC Immigration Enforcement Report.* http://trac.syr.edu/trains/latest/131/.

*Tucson Citizen.* "Mexico Draft Resolution Criticizing Border Fence at UN Human Rights Council." October 23, 2006.

Tucson Sector Border Patrol Public Information Office. "U.S. Border Patrol Launches Operation 'Be Alert.'" Press release. March 25, 2005. http://www.americanpatrol.com/cbp/press-releases/050325-billboard-tus_/050325Billboardtus_.html.

Uranga, Rachel. "Anti-Illegal Immigrant Groups Multiply." *Los Angeles Daily News,* August 12, 2006.

Van Der Werf, Martin, and Keoki Skinner, "Paramilitary Group That Caught Illegal Aliens Leaves Border Site." *Arizona Republic,* July 7, 1986.

Villa, Judi. "Arpaio's Migrant Arrests for Smuggling Hit 500." *Arizona Republic,* April 6, 2007.

——. "Migrant Worker Files Civil Suit Against Sheriff Arpaio." *Arizona Republic,* December 13, 2007.

Vina, Stephen R., Blas Nunez-Neto, and Alyssa Bartlett Weir. "Civilian Patrols Along the Border: Legal and Policy Issues." Congressional Research Service, Library of Congress, April 7, 2006, Order Code RL33353.

Vinyard, Ben. "Another Minuteman Update." April 4, 2005. http://www.whiterevolution.com/archives/20050404/another-minuteman-update.

Voices of Citizens Together. Newsletter. June 1996.

Waever, Ole. "Societal Security: The Concept." In *Identity, Migration and the New Security Agenda in Europe.* Edited by Ole Waever et. al. Copenhagen: Pinter, 1995.

——. "Securitization and Desecuritization." In *On Security.* Edited by Ronnie D. Lipschutz, 46–86. New York: Columbia University Press, 1995.

Wallace, J. P. "Anti-Illegal Immigration Propositions Get Thumbs-Up." KOLD News Channel 3, Tucson, Arizona, November 24, 2006. http://www.kold.com/global/story/asp?s=5659692&ClientType=Printable.

Walter Cronkite School of Journalism and KAET Public Television. Cronkite-Eight Poll. January 24, 2007. http://www.azpbs.org/horizon/poll/2007/1-24 -07.htm.

——. Cronkite-Eight Poll. June 26, 2007. http://www.azpbs.org/horizon/poll/2007/6-26-07.htm.

Watanabe, Teresa. "Human Rights Expert Examines Migrant Issues in L.A." *Los Angeles Times,* May 4, 2007.

Watson, Julie. "Armed U.S. Residents Are Patrolling Mexican Border on Their Own." *San Francisco Chronicle,* February 9, 2003.

Weisman, Jonathan. "With Senate Vote, Congress Passes Border Fence Bill." *Washington Post,* September 30, 2006.

Wells, Miriam J. "The Grassroots Reconfiguration of U.S. Immigration Policy." *International Migration Review* 38, no. 4 (winter 2004): 1308–1347.

White, Elizabeth. "Minuteman Project Plans Border-Watch Effort." *Houston Chronicle*, September 11, 2006.

Williams, Michael C. "Words, Images, Enemies: Securitization and International Politics." *International Studies Quarterly* 47 (2003): 511–531.

Wingette, Yvonne. "Arizona's Colleges Struggle to Enforce New tuition Statute." *Arizona Republic*, January 3, 2007.

Wisckol, Martin. "Event Turns Hostile." *Orange County Register*, May 26, 2005.

Wisckol, Martin. "Minutemen to Patrol Border in 4 States." *Orange Country Register*, March 30, 2006.

Women's Commission for Refugee Women and Children and Lutheran Immigration and Refugee Service. *Locking Up Family Values: The Detention of Immigrant Families*. Report. Women's Commission for Refugee Women and Children, 2007. http://www.womenscommission.org/pdf/famdeten.pdf.

Wood, Daniel B. "What 'Minutemen' Vigil Accomplished." *Christian Science Monitor*, May 2, 2005.

Wooldridge, Frosty. *Immigration's Unarmed Invasion*. Bloomington, Indiana: Author House, 2004.

Wyman, David S. "Former Senior Aide to Pat Buchanan Spoke at Holocaust-Deniers' Meeting." Press release. Institute for Holocaust Studies, December 16, 2004. http://www.wymaninstitute.org/press/2004-12-16.php.

Zaitchik, Alexander. " 'Christian' Nativism." *Southern Poverty Law Center Intelligence Report*, winter 2007. http://www.splcenter.org/intel/intelrepot/article.jsp?aid=724.

——. "Operation Sovereignty: A Bang, A Protest, and a Whimper." *Southern Poverty Law Center Intelligence Report*, winter 2007. http://www.splcenter.org/intel/intelrepot/article.jsp?sid=399.

Zeleny, Jeff. "Immigration Bill Prompts Some Menacing Responses." *New York Times*, June 27, 2007.

Zeskind, Leonard. "The New Nativism: The Alarming Overlap Between White Nationalists and Mainstream Anti-Immigrant Forces." *The American Prospect, Special Reports, Solving the Immigration Crisis*, November 2005, A15-A18.

# Index